FRUITFUL

DISCIPLESHIP

By
W. Edward Thiele

Insight Press

New Orleans, Louisiana

FRUITFUL DISCIPLESHIP

Published by Insight Press, Incorporated
P. O. Box 8369, New Orleans, Louisiana 70182

Printed in the United States of America

ISBN 0-914520-33-4

CONTENTS

Acknowledgments

I want to express my gratitude to the faculty, administration, and trustees of New Orleans Baptist Theological Seminary for the opportunity to formulate, teach, and write these thoughts. A sabbatical leave made the writing possible.

My wife, Catherine, was very encouraging and helpful throughout the project. My discipleship classes at the Seminary have provided the stimulation of interaction and dialogue as these subjects were presented. Connie McGee, my secretary, has done cheerfully the labor of putting the manuscript in final form.

Above all, I thank my Lord Jesus Christ for the calling to be His disciple and a disciplemaker. By His grace I shall continue to give my best to this high calling as long as I live.

PREFACE

Many books about discipleship have been written in recent years. It is as if we Christians had just discovered the subject. What has happened, however, is that more and more believers are becoming convinced that what Jesus had in His own mind and heart from the beginning of His mission was making disciples. The church has often concentrated on other things, but the intention of our Lord has never changed. He always intended to create a special people for Himself who would follow Him, obey His commands, hold to His teaching, and live His kind of life in the world.

I have written this book as one who earnestly desires to cooperate with Jesus in His plan and to encourage others to do so. A special opportunity is mine to teach seminary students, and I am strongly convinced that they should endeavor to be disciplemakers and trainers in disciplemaking, whatever their expression of Christian vocation may be. Some of them will become pastors, some teachers, evangelists, missionaries, writers, and other ministry positions in full-time or part-time endeavors. All of them should seek to be faithful disciples and to aid in the winning and developing of other disciples. I am writing with them particularly in mind.

My aim has been broader, however. All Christians need a thorough grasp of what it means to be a disciple of Jesus Christ, and they need to be prepared to introduce others to their Lord and Savior and to assist them in their growth as Christians. My hope is that some of these will find the book helpful in understanding and fulfilling their task. For too long non-professional Christians have failed to commit themselves to carrying out the purpose and plan of Jesus because of a misunderstanding that this was only for ordained or professional clergy. My persuasion is that this is the calling of every follower of Christ, both to be a disciple and to make disciples. One of my goals is to offer biblical support for this position.

Numerous Christian writers have provided books on discipleship for various audiences. I have read and found value in many of these. You have a right to ask how this book is different. I have tried to be comprehensive and biblical. Many sources have been used, and an attempt has been made to treat many aspects of the subject of discipleship. Also a deliberate effort has been made to avoid using proof texts out of context. Any preacher or writer is tempted to misuse verses of Scripture in order to make a point. I have been determined to avoid that error as much as possible and to respect the setting from which verses have been chosen.

My approach is pastoral. For twenty-eight years I functioned as a pastor of three Southern Baptist churches, two in Texas and one in Mississippi. I endeavored to lead the churches to be evangelistic so that persons would commit themselves to follow Jesus as Savior and Lord. Also, my aim was to lead the churches to be loving fellowships of believers in which lives would be transformed into the likeness of Christ. Although I have been a seminary professor for the last ten years, I have continued to offer pastoral care to the students and to churches which I served on a part-time basis.

My prayer is that through the use of this book God may be glorified, Christ exalted, and disciples strengthened for greater fruitfulness.

Unless otherwise indicated, the New International Version (NIV) is used for all the quoted references from the Bible.

PART ONE

GOD'S GOAL AND OUR DESIRE

God has always known what He wanted to accomplish on earth. In the opening chapters of Genesis His goal is revealed. He wanted male and female persons whom He created in His image or likeness to live in unity and to enjoy His blessings. Moreover, He wanted them to be fruitful managers of the resources He had given them. He intended for them to know and do good and not evil. Peaceful relationships with Him and with each other were included in His design. There was nothing wrong with His plan. It was very good!

But sovereign God elected to give freedom to these God-like ones and made it possible for them to choose to think, say, and do evil. Beginning with the first human pair, the choice of evil was made with disastrous consequences. That did not change God's goal, but the entrance of sin and disobedience changed the situation.

Only if sinners acknowledged their wrong choices as being contrary to God's plan and looked to God for forgiveness and help could they experience the sort of life and relationships for which they were made. Their sin made God's intervention necessary. His love made reconciliation possible. He extended a covenant to those willing to be His people. He would treat them with undeserved mercy if they would trust Him and follow His ways. He wanted to teach them obedience. His goal was for them to be a holy people. Here are His words through Moses:

> Now if you obey me fully and keep my covenant, then out of all nations you will be my treasured possession. Although the whole earth is mine, you will be for me a kingdom of priests and a holy nation (Ex. 19:5-6).

Therefore, we believe that Christian discipleship is in line with God's purpose expressed many centuries ago. God still wants faithful followers; He made a way through His Son, Jesus Christ, for the needed changes to take place.

The goal of God is never realized, however, apart from the cooperation of persons. Only as individuals desire what God offers to give and do will changes occur. The freedom and responsibility of human beings is awesome and real. Both salvation and sanctification are works of God and occur only when persons respond positively to the favorable opportunities He provides. This is a basic premise which underlies this book. No one achieves spiritual growth without wanting to and without turning to God for His activity of regeneration and maturation.

CHAPTER 1

FRUITFUL DISCIPLESHIP

Nine years of my childhood were spent in a citrus orchard. Our family lived two miles south of Mission, Texas, and had grapefruit trees on one side of the house and orange trees on the other. Besides that, we had banana trees and a papaya tree by the water well, and a fig tree by the barn. I love fruit, all kinds of fruit, everything about fruit—seeing fruit, picking fruit, eating fruit, drinking fruit juice. I would like to be growing fruit always.

A golden city with a golden street and jasper walls and gates of pearl is a lovely picture of heaven, but I like even better the tree of life on each side of the river of the water of life, "bearing twelve crops of fruit, yielding its fruit every month" (Rev. 22:1-2, NIV). That's paradise to me.

Although I was born and raised to be a fruit man, I was saved to become a fruitful disciple. You may not share my enthusiasm for fruit, but I am intent on helping you aspire to be fruitful in your discipleship. That is much more important.

God's Plan: Fruitfulness

God planned for His people to be fruitful. He called Abraham in order to bless him and to make him a blessing (Gen. 12:1-3). God made a covenant with Israel through Moses that if they would obey Him fully, He would make them a treasured possession, a kingdom of priests, and a holy nation (Ex. 19:3-6). The kingdom suggests the realm in which all God's people live under His authority as King. Priests were chosen for a sacred ministry. "Holy" means set apart for godly living. God was promising to make His people fruitful in living and serving, if they would be faithful to Him.

The first Psalm describes a good man whose delight is in the law of the Lord and who constantly meditates on it and lives by its revelation of righteousness: "He is like a tree planted by streams of water, which yields its fruit in season and whose leaf does not wither" (Ps. 1:3). He is a fruitful man. In contrast, the wicked "are like the chaff that the wind blows away" (Ps. 1:4).

One of the saddest songs in Scripture is Isaiah's lament over Israel for being an unproductive vineyard. God had done everything He could to prepare the nation to be a good crop, a fruitful vineyard. Then He looked for a crop of good grapes, but it yielded only bad fruit (Is. 5:2). The prophet helps us feel the disappointment of God when His people fail to respond properly to His loving initiative. "The vineyard of the Lord Almighty is the house of Israel, and the men of Judah are the garden of his delight. And he looked for justice, but saw bloodshed; for righteousness, but heard cries of distress" (Is. 5:7). The image of Israel as the vine is found in Ezek. 15:1-8 and 17:5-9; Hos. 10:1, and other places.

Another sad scene regarding God's chosen people is one depicted in the New Testament by Jesus cursing the fig tree that had leaves but no fruit. Probably Jesus was anticipating and subtly predicting the judgment that was coming on the fruitless religious leaders of Israel who refused to recognize His authority. The fig tree withered and died. Their opportunity for usefulness to God had been wasted by them. At least, if the disciples would continue to trust Him, they would be permitted to accomplish wonderful results (Mt. 21:18-22). Likewise, we who are willing to rely on Him in our time of discipleship may become truly fruitful. That is God's plan for us.

Defining Discipleship

Use of the word. The word for disciple in the Greek New Testament is *mathetes*, literally a learner, one who follows the teaching of a *didaskalos*, a teacher. The New Testament contains references to disciples of John the Baptist (Mt. 9:14); of the Pharisees (Mt. 22:16); of Moses (Jn. 9:28), and frequently of Jesus.[1]

In the Gospels, "disciples" is the word most often used of the Twelve (Mt. 10:1; Lk. 6:13, etc.), but not exclusively of them. Even prospects or inquirers might have been referred to as disciples. Some Jews who were called disciples quit following Him after a time and returned to their homes (Jn. 6:66). Joseph of Arimathea is spoken of as a secret disciple who came forward after Jesus' death to obtain His body from Pilate to give it proper burial (Jn. 19:38). We observe that the use of the word disciple did not always express the same kind or degree of

---

[1]K. H. Rengstorf, *mathetes*, *Theological Dictionary of the New Testament*, Gerhard Kittel, ed., vol. 4 (Grand Rapids: Eerdmans, 1967), 441 [hereafter referred to as *TDNT*].

commitment when used in the Gospels.

Historical Background. Greeks used the term "disciple" for one who studied the life and conduct, as well as the teaching of a teacher. This was most often a philosopher who instructed in itinerant fashion, but also a disciple might have been an apprentice in such skills as weaving, medicine, or music. Some teacher-philosophers like Epicurus required complete dependence and attachment of the disciples to themselves.[2]

The Old Testament has no direct parallel to the master-disciple relationship, but a consideration of the relationships of Moses and Joshua (Num. 27:15-23); of Elijah and Elisha (1 Kg. 19:19-21); and of Jeremiah and Baruch (Jer. 36:4-10) may provide useful insights. In each case God Himself is the Master and Teacher who illumined and guided His prophet, but God directed each to another man who would succeed or assist His messenger.

Rabbis were instructors in the Law (Torah) and its application during the New Testament era. The pupils learned from observation of the rabbi's conduct as well as from instruction and dialogue. Individuals or schools of disciples attached themselves to teachers for varying lengths of time. Sometimes a father-son relationship resulted.[3]

Comparison of Jesus with Other Rabbis. Although Jesus was occasionally addressed as "Rabbi" (Jn. 3:2, 26; 6:25, etc.), He was obviously different from other rabbis. While upholding the Law, He made fresh interpretations and application of it (Mt. 5:27-48). He associated publicly with women; normally rabbis could not do this. He devoted attention to children contrary to rabbinical custom. He ate and talked with sinners and tax-collectors—definitely forbidden to rabbis. He showed love and mercy to Gentiles also, and of course, no Jew was permitted to do that. Nevertheless, the establishment of the teacher-disciple method of instruction in Judaism prepared the way for Jesus' ministry to His disciples.[4]

The most important difference between Jesus and the practice of other rabbis, however, was the radical allegiance to His person and teachings

---

[2]Ibid., 416-22.

[3]Ibid., 432-37.

[4]John Hendrix and Lloyd Householder, eds., *The Equipping of Disciples* (Nashville: Broadman, 1977), 17. Cf. David Watson, *Called and Committed* (Wheaton: Harold Shaw, 1982), 6, 54; and Michael Griffiths, *The Example of Jesus* (Downers Grove, IL: InterVarsity, 1985).

that Jesus required. It was an unrivaled attachment to Himself which would shape the whole life of the disciple inside and out. Persecution was to be expected. Separation even from family members might occur, He told them. Love for Him would be shown by obedience to His commands. They were to place their lives under His authority and to be willing to be trained for a life of service in His name.

Disciples in the Gospels and Acts. A disciple of Jesus in the Gospels was one who was with Him as a learner and a follower, attaching to Him personally, adhering to His instruction, and generally doing what He commanded. A disciple was never perfect, but he was different from what he had been before following Jesus and different from others who did not share his allegiance to the Christ.

In Acts the term "disciple" has a meaning which better fits the current usage. Jesus had ascended to heaven, and there was no more visual following, physical contact, or audible reception of His teaching from His mouth. The Holy Spirit had been given to all believers, and they were joined together in spiritual fellowship. They worshiped, studied, prayed, and gave what they had (Acts 2:42-47). We cannot be sure how long this period lasted, but perhaps several years are covered in this summary.

Both men and women were called disciples after they had repented of their sins and trusted in Jesus Christ as Savior and Lord. For the first time the disciples were called Christians (Acts 11:26) and believers (Acts 4:32; 5:12; and 9:41). The term "disciple" was not used to indicate any superiority or maturity. Both new converts and mature apostles were described as disciples. When Paul was converted, he "spent several days with the disciples in Damascus" (Acts 9:19). Next, "he tried to join the disciples in Jerusalem" (Acts 9:26) and preached boldly among them. The apostles were effective in the leadership of the church in Jerusalem and the growth continued numerically and spiritually in Judea, Galilee, and Samaria (Acts 9:31). Paul and Barnabas were able to win "a large number of disciples" in Lystra, Iconium, and Antioch of Pisidia (Acts 14:21). Soon afterward, they returned to those cities "strengthening the disciples and encouraging them to remain true to the faith" (Acts 14:22).

The definition of disciple which I prefer is based primarily on the use of the term in Acts. The material in the Gospels is valuable, of course, but the history covered is the formative period which we could call the embryonic stage. Our understanding of what it means to follow Jesus is greatly influenced by Jesus' relation to His disciples in the day of His flesh, but the salvation of the first disciples and of all who have been saved since then was not completed until Jesus died, arose, ascended, and gave the Holy Spirit to all believers. Beginning on the day of Pentecost, we have had disciples who have been saved by repentance and faith and have acknowledged Jesus Christ as their Lord.

A Proposed Definition. *A disciple is a saved person who is learning to live under the lordship of Jesus Christ.* That means that every Christian is a disciple. A disciple may remain very immature for a long time after conversion. Paul addressed members of the church in Corinth as infants in Christ and worldly (1 Cor. 3:1). Jealousy and quarreling were offered as an evidence of it. The Apostle did not suggest that they were not spiritually regenerated, but only that they were immature. Many disciples are found in that condition today, but many mature Christians are also known by most of us. Disciples who display good attitudes, do deeds of service, live good moral lives and reveal faith in and love for Jesus are usually respected as mature disciples. They are not perfect, but they are learning what it means to obey Jesus as Lord in daily decisions. They are living for Him. They are in process and on the way to becoming what God desires for them to be.[5] The majority of believers may be in between, not infants and not mature, but disciples nevertheless, at some stage of growth, and perhaps temporarily plateaued.

Desirable Characteristics of a Disciple. Another way of describing a good disciple is in terms of desirable characteristics. The ideal ought to be kept in view. This approach is fine for goal-setting. Our vision of what a person acts like who is full-grown or complete as a disciple ought to be just as biblical and specific as possible.

Francis Cosgrove of the Navigators provided this profile of a disciple:

1. Puts Christ first in his life and is taking steps to separate from sin
2. Has a consistent daily devotional time and is developing a prayer life
3. Demonstrates faithfulness and a desire to learn and apply the Word
4. Manifests a heart for witnessing

---

[5]Christopher B. Adsit, *Personal Disciple-Making* (San Bernardino, CA: Here's Life Publishers, 1988), 34-35.

5. Attends church and maintains close ties with its fellowship, displaying love and unity
6. Demonstrates a servant heart
7. Is a learner—open and teachable
8. Is giving regularly and honoring God with one's finances
9. Will demonstrate the fruit of the Spirit by an attractive relationship with Christ and the fellowman and
10. Is seeking to determine and use spiritual gift(s).[6]

All of those characteristics are important, and we will discuss them in various ways throughout this book, but they are not used as an outline for our study. They do offer us a mental picture of a fruitful disciple.[7]

The first disciples of our Lord were not very perceptive (Mt. 13:36; 16:6-11; Jn. 16:16-20); not outstanding in their faith (Mt. 8:23-26); and not free of selfish ambition (Mk. 10:35-40). They sometimes lacked power (Mt. 17:14-21), discernment (Mk. 8:31-33), and courage (Jn. 20:19). They were, however, committed to Him, and, with the exception of Judas, they continued to be His followers.

Let's go back to the definition: A disciple is a saved person who is learning to live under the lordship of Jesus Christ. In spite of the sequence of events necessary when Christ called out His first disciples and trained them, gradually bringing them to a full commitment and then sending His Spirit to them, a person today becomes a disciple at the time of salvation. I do not understand the New Testament to teach salvation by spiritual osmosis or education. Discipleship begins at the point of one's conscious turning from sin to receive Jesus Christ as Savior and Lord. There is no discipleship until one believes in Jesus as the Christ, the crucified and risen Son of God, and surrenders to Him in order to learn to live the new life of a Christian. Granted, all the conversion experiences described in the New Testament are adult conversions. The process by which children born to Christian parents and reared in a church-related environment come to make their own commitment to Jesus

---

[6]Francis M. Cosgrove, Jr., *Essentials of New Life* (Colorado Springs: NavPress, 1978); Cf. *The Essentials of Discipleship* by the same author (Colorado Springs: NavPress, 1982).

[7]Cf. David Watson, *Called & Committed: World-Changing Discipleship* (Wheaton: Harold Shaw Publishers, 1982), 49-51. Watson goes into more detail and lists twenty-two characteristics.

is not recounted. Children may or may not have been included in the household or family conversions presented in Acts 10:33, 43-44 and 16:29-34. What we do know is that persons are saved individually when they make a sincere faith response to Jesus Christ and come into a right relationship with God. Some of the many important Scriptures which support this are Eph. 2:8-10; Rom. 3:21-24, 10:9-13; Heb. 7:25; Jn. 1:12-13, 3:16-18, 20:30-31; and 1 Jn. 5:11-13. The person who has been forgiven of sin and saved through trust in Jesus has become a disciple, learning to live under His lordship.

Baptism is intended to be a part of one's confession of faith and a public declaration that one's discipleship has begun. It is an act of obedience by a saved person to the new Lord over his life. One's life is under new management. One is beginning to learn to be "dead to sin but alive to God in Christ Jesus" (Rom. 6:11;Cf. 6:4; Col. 2:9-12). Baptism helps to picture that for that person and for others.

From Bible reading and prayer, from preaching and teaching, from supportive relationships with other believers, and from private and public worship, the new Christian can begin to grow and to develop a Christian lifestyle. As Herschel Hobbs wrote, "The emphasis is not on how much the pupil knows but on his willingness to turn himself over to the teacher for instruction."[8] Here "the teacher" is Jesus Christ. "One is not a Christian by believing that Jesus Christ is divine. Rather one becomes a Christian by believing in Jesus Christ—trusting one's life to Christ."[9] Saving faith is not mere intellectual assent; it is commitment. Commitment is essential to discipleship.[10] One cannot learn Christ's lordship without it. "The Christian life is quite distinct because it has a new direction, a new focus, a new center, a new outlook."[11] Jesus said, "If anyone would come after me, he must deny himself and take up his cross daily and follow me" (Lk. 9:23).

---

[8]Herschel Hobbs, *Fundamentals of Our Faith* (Nashville: Broadman Press), 110. See Eduard Schweizer, *Lordship and Discipleship* (London: SCM Press Ltd., 1960), 83.

[9]Morris Ashcraft, *Christian Faith and Beliefs* (Nashville: Broadman Press, 1984), 58.

[10]Daniel Holcomb, *Costly Commitment* (Nashville: Convention Press, 1978, rev.1987), 8-23.

[11]Ashcraft, 308.

Fruitfulness: Christ's Objective

One of the last recorded speeches of Jesus to His disciples found only in John's Gospel was on the subject of fruitfulness in discipleship. Jesus said, "I am the vine; you are the branches. If a man remains in me and I in him, he will bear much fruit; apart from me you can do nothing" (Jn. 15:5). Jesus is the Vine who produces fruit on the branches that are vitally connected to Him in faith and obedience. He is the only One who can make us fruitful. No exegesis of this section of Scripture will be attempted here. The major points in Jn. 15:1-16 are:

1. God is the gardener who prunes and seeks to produce as much fruit as possible on each branch (disciple) (vv. 1-2).
2. Jesus is the Vine who enables each branch (disciple) that is joined to Him to be fruitful (vv. 4-5).
3. Allowing His words to be in our minds and asking His help in prayer are ways to increase our fruitfulness (v. 7).
4. Fruitful discipleship brings the Father glory (v. 8).
5. Maintaining the love relationship with Jesus through obedience to His commands is essential to complete joy (vv. 9-11).
6. Love for others is a major means of fruitfulness and intimacy with Jesus (vv. 12-15).
7. Every disciple is chosen by Jesus to produce lasting fruit (v. 16).

Conclusion

Every saved person is a disciple, but obviously many are not very fruitful. They do not show much evidence that they are living under the lordship of Jesus. We will never have stronger churches without better disciples. The quality of discipleship in the pew will seldom rise higher than that in the pulpit. All church leaders, ordained and non-ordained, need to be committed to Jesus Christ as Lord in a life-long process of spiritual development that is reflected in increasing holiness and usefulness to the glory of God. Then, perhaps the other members will begin to comprehend that every saved person is called by Jesus to fruitful discipleship.

CHAPTER 2

LIVING UNDER HIS LORDSHIP

What one believes *about* Jesus Christ is crucial in discipleship. He is Lord. It is also essential to believe *in* Him. Everyone who believes in Him as Savior and Lord is entitled to assurance of eternal life. That person is saved by the grace of God. A new relationship with God and with Jesus Christ, His Son, has begun. To remain rightly related to Him in daily life involves learning to live under His lordship.

The Confession of the Early Church

Probably the earliest confession of believers coming into the church was "Jesus Christ is Lord."[1] Romans 10:9-10 seems to indicate this:

> That if you confess with your mouth, "Jesus is Lord," and believe in your heart that God raised him from the dead, you will be saved. For it is with your heart that you believe and are justified, and it is with your mouth that you confess and are saved.

Also, Paul wrote to young pastor Timothy, "Everyone who confesses the name of the Lord must turn away from wickedness" (2 Tim. 2:19). In his letter to the church in Corinth, the Apostle addressed it "to those sanctified in Christ Jesus and called to be holy, together with all those everywhere who call on the name of our Lord Jesus Christ . . . their Lord and ours" (1 Cor. 1:2). Furthermore, Phil. 1:10-11 stated God's ultimate aim in exalting Jesus to the highest place: "that at the name of Jesus every knee should bow in heaven and on earth and under the earth, and every tongue confess that Jesus Christ is Lord, to the glory of God the Father."

Jesus accepted and was pleased with Peter's confession that He was the Christ (Messiah), the Son of the living God (Mt. 16:16). Then, after Jesus' resurrection and ascension, Peter, under the power and leadership of the Holy Spirit, proclaimed Jesus "both Lord and Christ" (Acts 2:36). The church in Jerusalem was made up of those who accepted His message, repented of their sins, and were baptized (Acts 2:38-41). Paul

---

[1]F. F. Bruce, *The Acts of the Apostles* (Chicago: InterVarsity Press, 1952), 96.

later affirmed, "No one can say 'Jesus is Lord,' except by the Holy Spirit" (1 Cor. 12:3). When we make that confession of faith today, we are on solid biblical ground. We are in step with those who belonged to the first churches on earth.

The Biblical Background of "Lord"

What did the title "Lord" mean in the first century A.D.? An examination of the use of the word in both the Old and New Testaments is necessary to understand what it meant to the first Christians.

The Greek term for lord is *kurios* and means one with authority and power.[2] It was used of an owner or a master as in the parable which Jesus told about the workers who were hired to work in the vineyard by the *kurios* (owner) in Mt. 20:8. Another use is as a title of respect like "sir." The son in the parable of Jesus who was ordered to work in his father's vineyard replied, "I will, sir (*kurie*)" (Mt. 21:29). In passages like Eph. 6:5-9, *kuriois* (pl.) is used to refer to masters in distinction from their slaves. All of these uses are suggestive for us since we are to respect Jesus, to belong to Him, and to serve Him.

In the Hebrew Old Testament *El* and its plural *Elohim* are the words most often used for God. The plural when used for the one true God indicated majesty. *Yahweh* is the name God chose by which to reveal Himself to Israel when He said to Moses, "This is what you are to say to the Israelites: 'I AM has sent me to you'" (Ex. 3:14). The name revealed the eternal existence and independence of God. Israel regarded it as God's holiest name and later became reluctant to speak or write it. *Adon* or its plural *Adonai* were normally used in place of *Yahweh*.[3] Both terms were translated "Lord" and emphasized His ownership and authority. References to deity by the compound name "the Lord God" are numerous.[4]

The Greek translation of *Adon* is *Kurios* in the Septuagint (Old Testament translation in Greek from the interbiblical period). This helps us understand the importance of Jesus being referred to as *Kurios* (Lord) since *Kupios* was used by Greek-speaking Jews in the New Testament era

---

[2]*TDNT*, III, 1041.

[3]*TDNT*, III, 1059.

[4] Robert L. Hamblin and William H. Stephens, *The Doctrine of Lordship* (Nashville: Convention Press, 1990), 23-25.

to refer to God. Jesus' disciples were consciously calling Him by their name for God.[5]

The writers of the Gospels employed this term "Lord" in referring to Jesus as well as to God. An angel announced His birth to the shepherds: "Today in the town of David a Savior has been born to you; he is Christ the Lord" (Lk. 2:11). John the Baptist understood that his mission was to prepare the way for the Lord (Mt. 3:11). Jesus asserted His authority over the Sabbath by telling the Pharisees, "The Son of Man is Lord even of the Sabbath" (Mk. 2:28). Sometimes a form of *Kurios* (Lord) is used by others to address Jesus conversationally with a term of respect, and sometimes Jesus used the term *Kurios* (Lord) in His parables to indicate an owner or master with authority over others. He also suggested the right and wrong use of it by His disciples in referring to Himself as He called for obedience to His teaching (Lk. 6:46).

The use of the title Lord by Jesus' followers was to indicate faith in Him in several instances. The blind man who was given sight by Jesus used "Lord" as he confessed his belief and worshiped Him (Jn. 9:38). Martha likewise addressed Him as Lord when she confessed her faith in Jesus as the Christ, the Son of God (Jn. 11:27). Jesus told the disciples at the last Passover, "You call me Teacher and Lord, and rightly so, for that is what I am" (Jn. 13:13). Particularly after the resurrection of Jesus it is obvious that *Kurios* (Lord) is used of Him by the New Testament writers. Thomas, reluctant to accept the resurrection at first, saw the risen Christ and exclaimed, "My Lord and my God!" (Jn. 20:28). Also, the two disciples on the Emmaus road, after they had been with the risen One, reported to the other disciples, "It is true! The Lord has risen and has appeared to Simon" (Lk. 24:34).

In the book of Acts, the message is that God has made Jesus Lord by raising Him from the dead (Acts 2:36; 4:33; 10:36, 39-40). Of course, He was already Lord, but God made His identity clear and His authority obvious, putting His approval upon all Jesus had said and done by raising Him up from death after the crucifixion.

By the time Paul wrote his epistles, "Lord" had become a part of the name so that "the Lord Jesus Christ" was frequently used. Also, "the Lord" is cited to distinguish Jesus from God the Father (1 Cor. 1:3; Gal. 1:3; Eph. 1:2-3).

We speak and write and sing of Jesus as our Lord in a spirit of

---

[5]Ibid., 25.

reverence with the whole biblical revelation before us. He is God to us, and yet distinct from God the Father in that as His Son He was completely obedient in revealing the truth in His life and teachings, and in dying an atoning death for our sins in perfect harmony with God's will. We worship Him as the living Lord and are committed to learn to live under His lordship and to witness of Him to others so that they too may do likewise.

Evidence to Support Jesus' Lordship

The New Testament writers used the name "Lord" of Jesus although it had been previously reserved by the Jews for reference only to the One God. We should, therefore, take seriously our use of the name of Jesus in worship and witness. Also, we should be able to defend the propriety of calling Jesus by that name and of giving Him supreme authority over our lives.

Although they are not set together in any one place in Scripture, the supporting truths are presented. We are not left without evidence that it is altogether right for us to worship and obey Jesus Christ as Lord. We are not just following tradition. Some of this evidence is:

His Claims for Himself

He called Himself the Son of Man with apparent reference to the use of that title by Daniel who had a vision of a son of man being led into God's presence where

He was given authority, glory and sovereign power; all peoples, nations and men of every language worshipped him. His dominion is an everlasting dominion that will not pass away, and his kingdom is one that will never be destroyed (Dan. 7:14).

Also Jesus welcomed being called Christ (Messiah), the Son of God (Mt. 16:16, Jn. 1:41; 11:27); and when interrogated by the chief priest who demanded, "Tell us if you are the Christ, the Son of God," Jesus replied, "Yes, it is as you say" (Mt. 26:63-64). Furthermore, He called Himself "the way, the truth, and the life" (Jn. 14:6) and referred to Himself as Lord (Jn. 13:13; Mt. 7:21-23) and King on the throne of judgment (Mt. 25:34, 37) with the intention of affirming His authority over the disciples.

The Way That He Taught

Jesus proved to others by the uniqueness and forcefulness of His teaching that He was the divine Lord. The content as well at the delivery of His lessons were compelling. He quoted the Law of Moses saying, "You have heard that it was said . . . But I tell you . . ." (Mt. 5:21-22, 27-28, 31-32, 38-39, 43-44). He taught with original authority, and this amazed the people (Mk. 1:22; Mt. 7:28-29).

The Miracles That He Did

There are thirty-five individual miracles of Jesus recorded in the Gospels and several summary statements attesting to clusters of miracles which He also performed. They include healing miracles, raising the dead, feeding thousands, casting out evil spirits, calming the storm, and walking on the water. Jesus told Philip and the other disciples, "Believe me when I say that I am in the Father and the Father is in me; or at least believe on the evidence of the miracles themselves" (Jn. 14:11). When John the Baptist in prison sent a query to Jesus seeking reassurance that He was the promised Messiah, Jesus told John's disciples to go back and tell him about the healing miracles, the raising of the dead, and the gospel being preached to the poor (Mt. 11:4-5). Although John's Gospel recounts only seven selected miracles, each of them is a sign (*semeion*) and, "He thus revealed his glory, and his disciples put their faith in him" (Jn. 2:11).

His Authority to Forgive Sin

Although Jesus did not say much about His forgiving sins, what He did say is very important. He healed a paralytic by first saying, "Take heart, son; your sins are forgiven" (Mt. 9:2). Some teachers of the Law thought He was blaspheming since only God can forgive sins, but Jesus told them He had said those words to reveal to them "that the Son of Man has authority on earth to forgive sins" (Mt. 9:6). In addition, He demonstrated forgiveness toward sinners like the woman of Samaria (John 4), Zacchaeus (Lk. 19:1-10), and the woman who wet Jesus' feet with her tears, wiped them with her hair, kissed them and poured perfume on them. Jesus declared, "Therefore, I tell you, her many sins have been forgiven—for she loved much. But he who has been forgiven little loves little." Then Jesus said to her, "your sins are forgiven" (Lk. 7:47-48).

His Fulfillment of Old Testament Prophecies

Jesus studied the Scriptures to learn more about His purpose and fulfilled the prophecies concerning Himself. He announced His mission when He read Is. 61:1-2 in the Nazareth synagogue and told the hearers, "Today this scripture is fulfilled in your hearing" (Lk. 4:21). He entered Jerusalem on Palm Sunday riding a donkey because Zech. 9:9 foretold that kind of coming of the righteous king who brought salvation (Mt. 21:1-11). Because Jesus called God His Father, the Jews persecuted Him. Jesus responded,

> You diligently study the Scriptures because you think that by them you possess eternal life. These are the scriptures that testify about me, yet you refuse to come to me to have life (Jn. 5:39-40).

They should have let the prophecies lead them to receive Him as the Lord.

Then, we have the account of the resurrection appearance of Jesus when He chided the two disciples for not believing all that the prophets had spoken. "And beginning with Moses and all the Prophets, he explained to them what was said in all the Scriptures concerning himself" (Lk. 24:27).

His Living Without Sin

We believe we have a sufficient record of His life to know that He never yielded to temptation. His mastery over Satan is best seen in the temptation record which two Gospels contain (Mt. 4:1-11; Lk. 4:1-13). On another occasion He challenged His Jewish antagonists by asking, "Can any of you prove me guilty of sin?" (Jn. 8:46). The writer of Hebrews sums up the universal testimony of the Christian community thus: "For we do not have a high priest who is unable to sympathize with our weaknesses, but we have one (Jesus the Son of God) who has been tempted in every way, just as we are—yet was without sin" (Heb. 4:15). We need such a Lord to help us when we are tempted.

His Dying and Rising Again

Luke tells how the faithful women from Galilee came to the tomb at the first daylight after the Sabbath to anoint the body "of the Lord Jesus" (Lk. 24:3). Although they did not find His body, they met two angels who reminded them how Jesus had predicted His death and resurrection

(Lk. 24:4-8). Also, the conversation of the risen Jesus with the two disciples on the Emmaus road caused them to report to the assembly of disciples, "The Lord has risen" (Lk. 24:34). When the hundred and twenty believers came together in Jerusalem after the resurrection and ascension to pray, Peter led them to replace Judas. He insisted the apostle selected had to be one of the men who had been with them the whole time the Lord Jesus was among them and was a witness of His resurrection (Acts 1:15-22). The main thrust of Peter's sermon on the day of Pentecost was that Jesus, after being nailed to the cross, was raised from the dead by God. God had made this Jesus "both Lord and Christ" (Acts 2:22-36). Paul explained that lordship was central to the purpose of Jesus' death and resurrection: "For this very reason, Christ died and returned to life so that he might be the Lord of both the dead and the living" (Rom. 14:9). Only Jesus by His death and resurrection earned the right to be worshiped and served as our Lord.

The Issue of Authority

All authority relates to persons. It is the right and power of a person or persons to compel action or thought in others. Authority may be conferred or earned. In human experience it is seldom absolute. One is free to accept or reject an expressed authority while accepting the consequences of the choice.

We live in a world of authorities, such as those in police, government, school, employment, and religion. Some authorities have more power over us than others. The well-being of individuals is conditioned to a large extent by their ability and willingness to relate themselves properly to the authorities in their lives.

God is the name commonly used for the highest authority in life. This is a religious concept, but the authority extends over all of life. He is referred to as the Lord or as the Lord God. The authority is absolute. To say that Jesus is Lord is to say that He is God—co-equal and co-eternal. He created all things (Jn. 1:3; Col. 1:15-16). Jesus said, "I am the Alpha and the Omega, the Beginning and the End" (Rev. 21:6). He told His disciples just before giving the Great Commission, "All authority in heaven and on earth has been given to me" (Mt. 28:18). He deserves absolute obedience. God conferred that authority on the Son. God highly exalted Him to the highest place (Phil. 2:9; Acts 2:33). In a special sense also, Jesus earned that authority over us by His perfect obedience to the

Father. He was obedient in servant form to death, "even death on a cross!" (Phil. 2:8). We were bought at a price (1 Cor. 6:20). "If we live, we live to the Lord; and if we die, we die to the Lord. So whether we live or die, we belong to the Lord" (Rom. 14:8). Our lives are to give evidence of His ownership.

The church is a body of members of which Jesus is the head. The church's calling is to proclaim supremacy for Him in everything (Col. 1:18). Obvious to all should be the lordship of Jesus Christ in every aspect of the church, particularly its worship, fellowship, witness and service. The church has one Lord (Eph. 4:5). That is a key to its unity. Any conflict arising from members seeking authority for themselves over others in the church is terribly inappropriate. Those of us called to leadership in the church should be acutely aware of His leadership of us and of our accountability to Him.

The issue of authority is also very personal. Every Christian has called on the name of the Lord to be saved (Rom. 10:13). He or she has been called by the Lord to follow. As Francis M. Cosgrove, Jr., wrote, "The Lordship of Christ is the daily submission and surrender of our entire self to the authority and leadership of Jesus Christ, recognizing his sovereign right to rule preeminently over us."[6] The initial commitment to Jesus as Savior and Lord needs to be backed-up by daily recommitment. He calls for daily cross bearing (Lk. 9:23), co-crucifixion. Temptations come in the form of daily opportunities to think, speak, and act in ways contrary to the will of our Lord. Any disobedience of His commands and rejection of the leadership of His Spirit is sinful refusal to live under His lordship. We are still and will remain sinners throughout our lives, but we should have settled the issue of authority with Him as our Lord.

Lordship Salvation

A provocative question which has been debated by various Christian leaders in recent years is whether or not a person must be committed to the lordship of Jesus Christ in order to be saved. James Montgomery Boice in *Christ's Call to Discipleship*[7] and John MacArthur in *The*

---

[6]Francis M. Cosgrove, Jr., *The Essentials of Discipleship* (Colorado Springs: NavPress, 1980), 37.

[7]James Montgomery Boice, *Christ's Call to Discipleship* (Chicago: Moody, 1986).

Gospel According to Jesus[8] say "yes." Since Jesus is both Savior and Lord, only the person who accepts His salvation and surrenders to Him as Lord is saved, they contend. They see no division between conversion and discipleship. A person is saved from sin to become a disciple of Jesus the Lord. Both the salvation and the calling from the Lord to be disciples are a work of grace on God's part.

On the other hand, Zane Hodges in *Absolutely Free*[9] and Charles Ryrie in *So Great Salvation*[10] hold that to require submission to Christ's lordship as a condition for salvation is to add to and thus distort the doctrine of salvation by grace alone. Acceptance of the truths of the gospel that Christ died, was buried, and rose again is what is important.[11] By believing the gospel, a person is saved because of the grace of God. Surrender, even if a part of believing, is a human work that dilutes grace.[12] Nevertheless, Ryrie states that "an element of commitment must be present in trusting Christ for salvation."[13]

Where does fruit come into the picture? "Fruit . . . furnishes evidence of saving faith."[14] Both sides agree that fruitfulness should be expected after the saving work of grace. Ryrie lists a Christlike character (Gal. 5:22-23; 2 Pet. 1:5-8), a life characterized by good works (Col. 1:10; Phil. 1:22), a faithful witness (Rom. 1:13; 1 Cor. 16:15), praise and grateful confession (Heb. 13:15), and money generously given (Rom. 15:28; Phil. 4:17) as fruit. The changes in one's life should become apparent after one receives Christ as Savior.[15] MacArthur agrees, saying, "Professing Christians utterly lacking the fruit of true righteousness will find no biblical basis for assurance they are saved" (1 Jn. 2:4).[16]

No further attempt will be made to explore this debate. I do affirm it as an important discussion which doubtless will continue. We must all decide what constitutes saving faith, what indicates a genuine experience of God's grace, and when discipleship begins.

---

[8]John MacArthur, *The Gospel According to Jesus* (Grand Rapids: Zondervan, 1988).
[9]Zane Hodges, *Absolutely Free* (Dallas: Redencio Viva, 1989).
[10]Charles Ryrie, *So Great Salvation* (Wheaton, IL: Victor, 1989).
[11]Ibid., 39-40.
[12]Ibid., 18.
[13]Ibid., 121.
[14]Ibid., 47.
[15]Ibid., 98.
[16]MacArthur, 23; Cf. 33.

Submission and Obedience

Living under the lordship of Jesus Christ requires the attitude of submission and the practice of obedience. Disciple-learners must remain teachable. No progress in discipleship will happen if the disciples are not trainable. Mary of Bethany sitting at the feet of Jesus listening to His teaching is a picture to carry in our hearts (Lk. 10:39). Our Lord told the Twelve, "A student is not above his teacher, nor a servant above his master" (Mt. 10:24).

Childlikeness is an asset, not a liability. It is not the opposite of maturity, but a requirement for it. Jesus was answering the disciples' question about greatness in the kingdom when He called a child to stand before them and said,

> I tell you the truth, unless you change and become like little children you will never enter the kingdom of heaven. Therefore, whoever humbles himself like this child is the greatest in the kingdom of heaven (Mt. 18:3-4).

The Lord can rule in the life of one who is sufficiently submissive to His authority. He has much to teach the one who has a heart hungry to learn. He is stymied by anyone who is too proud, independent, and self-reliant to come to Him with openness in anticipation of receiving direction from Him.

Obedience to the Lord's commands is another aspect of discipleship. His lordship refers to His right to command us. He is our Master and Owner. He knows and desires what is best for us. He would not tell us to do anything that was not for our good. "No, Lord" is a contradiction. Calvin Miller wrote, "The issue of every disciple is whether or not he or she shall have a Lord or be one."[17]

A search of the Gospels reveals some specific commands: "Follow me" (Mt. 9:9); "love the Lord your God with all your heart and with all your soul and with all your mind and with all your strength" (Mk. 12:30); "love your neighbor as yourself" (Mk. 12:31); "do not judge" (Mt. 7:1); "seek first his kingdom and his righteousness" (Mt. 6:33); and there are many more. His commands often have a promise attached

---

[17]Calvin Miller, *The Table of Inwardness* (Downers Grove, IL: InterVarsity, 1984), 79.

(Mt. 7:7-8; 28:20). We should not look only for those statements of imperative command. Other things He instructs us to do by pointing to the merit of them and reward for them, like the Beatitudes (Mt. 5:3-12). The point is, a disciple should be so anxious to obey the Lord that he or she hunts in the Word all the time for commands to keep and teachings to follow.

The rest of the New Testament also is full of commands from the Lord, stated and implied. If the mandate comes through Paul or Peter, for instance, it is no less His word to us. Passages like Rom. 12:9-21, need our attention for the rest of our lives. The Epistles are full of exhortations to believers which are to be treated as commands. One learns to live under Christ's lordship by daily obedience.

The home is the basic training camp for learning to take orders. The heritage which God desires for every child is to be trained by loving parents and taught the joy of obedience to reasonable requirements. "Children, obey your parents in the Lord, for this is right" (Eph. 6:1) is a universal command which, if properly carried out in a supportive environment, affords the best preparation possible for learning to trust and obey the Lord.

My school experiences were rich in opportunities to learn to follow the direction of another. The classroom, bands, choirs, athletic teams, and military organizations are some of the environments in which I was drilled at taking orders. Whether the leader used a voice, a baton or a whistle, the unit functioned effectively together if there was recognition of the leader's authority followed by obedience. There is no place to learn what Jesus proposes to do for a person but in the School of Christ.[18]

Devotion is closely linked to obedience in our following Jesus. "If you love me, you will obey what I command," the Master said (Jn. 14:15). Just as Jesus showed His love for the Father through obedience, we are called to show our love for Him the same way. The condition He gives for remaining in a close love relationship with Him is obedience to His teaching (Jn. 14:23; 15:10).

Submission to His loving authority with a teachable spirit comes first.[19] Then, daily obedience to His commands as an expression of our

---

[18]For a fuller development of this idea see W. F. McDowell, *In the School of Christ* (New York: Fleming H. Revell, 1910), 90.

[19]Juan Carlos Ortiz, *Disciple* (Carol Stream, IL: Creation House, 1975), 22, 111.

love for Him follows.[20] We will learn to be good disciples of our Lord if we have these two elements in place.

Practical Application

The proper stewardship of time is an important application to make of Jesus' lordship in our lives. Time is the gift of God measured out to us one moment at a time. We are accountable for our proper use of the days God gives us.

Jesus modeled good time management for us. Like Him, we must try to use our hours to glorify God. This involves setting God-given priorities for our lives. Then we can plan wisely how to use each day. Surely, we shall want to ask God's blessings on our plans and to seek His power and guidance as we try to carry them out. When we have done the best we can to carry out our plans, we must trust God for the results.

The only way Jesus can master our lives is for us to yield them to Him, one moment at a time. A holy life can be lived by a succession of holy days. If we do not allow Him to be the Lord of our days, we will never realize true discipleship.

Study Questions

1. What does it mean to confess Jesus as Lord?
2. How many commands of Jesus can you readily recall?
3. Do we earn God's love by our obedience?
4. Can we show love for Christ without obeying His teachings?
5. What is the relation between the authority of Jesus and other authority figures in your life?

---

[20]Elizabeth Eliot, *Discipline: The Glad Surrender* (New York: Fleming H. Revell, 1982).

CHAPTER 3

THE EXAMPLE OF JESUS

Disciples of Jesus can know what kind of persons they are destined to become. The qualities that should mark us as His followers are those which we find in His life. Ours is an incarnational faith. "The Word became flesh and made His dwelling among us" (Jn. 1:14). As He embodied God to us, we are called to embody Him to others. We are not saved by His example. To have His example without His saving power would only frustrate us. He saved us, however, so that we might be able to grow into His likeness. The sort of life He lived we may learn to live, and the measure of our spiritual growth is our likeness to Him. Developing Christlikeness is the work of the Holy Spirit in the yielded believer. It is never a human achievement.

All human beings are created in the image of God. However, sin has so disfigured persons that they may bear little resemblance to Him. Redemption restores the capacity to grow in His likeness. In bringing us redemption, Jesus also brought us the moving picture of God's likeness in human form (Jn. 14:7-9). When we repented of sin and trusted Him as Savior, we were started on the path of becoming like Him. As we become increasingly familiar with the Christ of the Gospels, we are permitted to see how we will turn out ultimately; we will be like Him (1 Jn. 3:2). We also see what kind of spiritual formation should be happening in us now.

Jesus in Relation to the Father

Jesus had a subordinate relationship to God the Father during His earthly ministry. He was submissive to the Father in a way similar to the way we are to be submissive to Jesus in our discipleship. That is a part of the self-emptying (*kenosis*) He demonstrated. The fifth, sixth, and eighth chapters of John contain most of Jesus' explanation of this relationship. For example, He said:

I tell you the truth, the Son can do nothing by himself; he can only do what he sees his Father doing, because whatever the Father does the Son also does (Jn. 5:19).

By myself I can do nothing; I judge only as I hear, and my judgment is just, for I seek not to please myself but him who sent me (Jn. 5:30).

Do not work for food that spoils, but for food that endures to eternal life, which the Son of man will give you. On him God the Father has placed his seal of approval (Jn. 6:27).

When you have lifted up the Son of Man, then you will know that I am the one I claim to be and that I do nothing on my own but speak just what the Father has taught me. The one who sent me is with me; he has not left me alone, for I always do what pleases him (Jn. 8:28-29).

Even His choice of the title Son of Man for self-reference may be an indication of His submissive role in relation to the Father. His prayers and temptations also suggest the nature of this relationship. His authority was received (Mt. 28:18). Jesus was dependent on the Father and submissive to the Father. He obeyed His commands (Jn. 15:10).

The point is, Jesus was not just putting on a demonstration for us. He truly lived the example which we are called to follow. He showed us how to live for God relying on the power and guidance God gives. He modeled pleasing God and obeying His commands. While accomplishing our salvation, He also gave us a perfect example to strive to follow.

Features of Jesus' Example

Jesus' boyhood seems a natural place to begin searching for features of His example. While we have scant biblical material about the youth of Jesus, the summary supplied in Luke's account is a valuable statement of **balanced growth**: "Jesus grew in wisdom and stature, and in favor with God and men" (Lk. 2:52). Physical, mental, spiritual and social development was taking place. Here is a norm by which to gauge growth among disciples of all ages. Balanced progress in every phase of life is a goal in discipleship.

The **baptism** of Jesus was a public commitment to the will of God. The Jordan River immersion was a sign to John, and a testimony to all, that Jesus was committed to carrying out the Father's plan. His answer to John's stated reluctance to baptize Him was, "Let it be so now; it is proper for us to do this to fulfill all righteousness" (Mt. 3:15). We are called not only to seek baptism as a confession of faith and act of obedience (Mt. 28:19-20; Acts 2:38, 41), but also as a sign of our desire to carry out God's will.

Memorization of Old Testament Scriptures must have been an important part of Jesus' discipleship as He grew up and as He prepared for His Messianic role in young adulthood. He was able to draw upon these Scriptures in the difficult time of temptation in the desert. Matthew 4:1-11 records how our Lord recited Scriptures to the devil when each attack was mounted against Him (Dt. 8:3; 6:16; Ps. 91:11-12). At other times Jesus quoted the Law in His teaching (Mt. 5:21, 27, 31, 33, 38) or used it in interpreting events as they happened (Jn. 13:18; 15:25). If the Master of persons utilized memorization of Bible verses, His disciples still must be encouraged to do so.

Early in His ministry, Jesus set an example for us in **public worship**. He went to the synagogue in Nazareth on the sabbath. He had often attended there. He read the Scriptures aloud from the scroll of Isaiah (Is. 61:1-2). When He had finished, He declared the promises of that passage fulfilled (Lk. 4:16-21). The habits of public assembly for worship, public reading of Scripture, and finding God's plan for our lives with reference to its message are a part of the example He set for all of us.

Jesus set a splendid example for us in **prayer**. He sometimes prayed alone (Mt. 14:23), sometimes publicly (Jn. 11:41-42). He prayed before important decisions and occasionally prayed all night (Lk. 6:12-13), or early in the morning (Mk. 1:35). Jesus prayed for others (Jn. 17:6-26) as well as for Himself (Mt. 26:39-43). He taught others to pray (Lk. 11:1-4). One of the best ways for any of us to learn to pray is by praying with others. Jesus by His example, nevertheless, is our first teacher in prayer.

A positive model of **time management** is given by Jesus. He moved with deliberation through three years of public ministry. His pace was unhurried, never frantic. We feel His poise as He prepared to heal a blind man, saying to His disciples:

As long as it is day, we must do the work of him who sent me. Night is coming when no one can work. While I am in the world, I am the light of the world (Jn. 9:4-5).

He obviously consulted the Father about the timing for various events in

His ministry. His first reply to His mother's request for Him to do something about the lack of wine for the wedding feast in Cana was, "My time has not yet come" (Jn. 2:4). On the other hand, as He prayed on the eve of His crucifixion, He said, "Father, the time has come" (Jn. 17:1). The many miracles, the teachings, the conversations, the crucifixion, resurrection, and ascension all were accomplished at the right time.

Jesus practiced **lifestyle evangelism**. He told Pilate during His trial, "For this reason I was born, and for this I came into the world, to testify to the truth" (Jn. 19:37). Nicodemus came to Him at night and Jesus told him how he could enter the kingdom of God. He met the Samaritan woman at noon at the well and told her how to have living water and never be thirsty again. He called four men to discipleship while they were taking care of their fishing business (Mk. 1:16-20); another was called while at his tax collector's booth (Mk. 2:14). Sometimes He invited inquirers for conversation to the place where He was staying (Jn. 1:37-39), and at other times He went to their homes (Lk. 19:1-10; Mt. 9:9-13). He set an example of witnessing on the move, wherever He was, and people were willing to listen. He began at their current level of understanding and interest and proceeded to share with them the truths that could radically alter their lives. There was no "hard sell." He gave them the truth and left them free to decide. Relational, marketplace, friendship, or lifestyle evangelism was what Jesus used.

Christ also **modeled counting the cost** of faithfulness to God just as He taught His followers to do. He spoke often to His disciples of how He would suffer and be killed in Jerusalem (Mk. 8:31; 9:30-31; 10:32-34). As the end drew near, "Jesus resolutely set out for Jerusalem" (Lk. 9:51). He referred to His death by crucifixion as a cup He had to drink and a baptism He had to be baptized with (Mk. 10:38). He was ready. He had already counted the cost. When we are faced with the demands of a costly discipleship, we may be encouraged by Jesus' example.

Obviously, **loving others** was a regular practice of Jesus. His major accent on loving relationships would likely have been disregarded if He had not demonstrated what He taught. He said,

A new command I give you: Love one another. As I have loved you, so you must love one another. By this all men will know that you are my disciples, if you love one another (Jn. 13:34-35).

The love of Jesus was expressed in compassionate action, not in gushy sentimentality. His healing miracles were evidence of His care as well as His power. The accounts that mention His taking the sick by the hand are particularly striking statements of His loving manner (Mk. 1:29-31; 8:22-26) and He even raised a dead girl back to life by taking her hand (Mk. 5:40-42). Jesus showed love, not only by miraculously helping, but by His gentle way. At times, however, His love was expressed in strong confrontation; for instance, when He cast out demons (Mk. 1:23-26; 9:25-26), or defended Himself against teachers of the Law (Mk. 3:22-30; 7:5-13), or corrected the disciples for their error in rejecting children (Mk. 10:13-16). The washing of the disciples' feet, even Judas's, was surely one of His greatest acts of love (Jn. 13:1-17). It was on that occasion that He told them, "I have set you an example that you should do as I have done for you" (Jn. 13:15).

Jesus' death on the cross is for all time the supreme act of love. He told the disciples on the night before His crucifixion, "Greater love has no one than this, that he lay down his life for his friends" (Jn. 15:13). He went on to offer Himself in sacrifice for the world's sins—His body and blood—as He said at the last supper (Mt. 26:26-28). Then, while suspended on the cross, Jesus demonstrated how to love one's enemies. He prayed for the executioners as they cast lots for His clothes, "Father, forgive them, for they do not know what they are doing" (Lk. 23:34). The better we know the gospel stories the more we will be able to emulate the love of the Lord in our life situations.

Servanthood was modeled by Jesus for His disciples. He saw Himself fulfilling the Servant prophecies of Isaiah.[1] He told His disciples, "I am among you as one who serves" (Lk. 22:27). Instead of trying to get others to wait on you and serve you, Jesus taught, you should look for ways to serve them. He demonstrated that lifestyle of service. He knew it was essential to His ministry. He said, "The Son of Man did not come to be served, but to serve, and to give his life as a ransom for many" (Mk. 10:45). Read anywhere in the Gospels and you will find the Savior serving—serving the sick, the fearful, the demon-possessed, the hungry, even the dead and the mourners, and finally serving all of us sinners by His death and resurrection. To be His disciple today is to be a servant to all whom we can serve. God supplies the gifts, shows us the needs

---

[1]Jesus particularly identified with the Servant prophecies in Is. 42:1-9; 49:1-7; 53:1-12.

around us, and supplies the guidance and power of the Spirit so that we can minister to others for His glory.

Other incidents in the earthly life of Jesus could be cited to complete the model for disciples. You may prefer to sketch out the model topically, such as His example in humility, gentleness, joyfulness, peacefulness, and simplicity. Admittedly, I have painted with broad strokes just to implant the concept that in our discipleship we are to seek to know and follow the example of Jesus. None of us will succeed perfectly, but we are called to try. As John wrote, "Whoever claims to live in him must walk as Jesus did" (1 Jn. 2:6).[2] Michael J. Wilkins's statement is: "To be a disciple of Jesus Christ means living a fully human life in this world in union with Jesus Christ and growing in conformity to his image."[3]

Following Jesus

Was it only the first disciples who could follow Jesus because they could see and hear and touch Him? It is clear that Jesus called out at least some of those disciples with an explicit command, "Follow me" (Mt. 4:19; 9:9), and they left what they were doing and physically followed Him. It was also an indication of commitment to Him and to learning and practicing His teaching. If they did not know it initially, they soon learned that theirs must be an unrivaled attachment to Him (Lk. 14:26-27, 33). The Twelve and the women from Galilee remained in close proximity to Jesus during much of His ministry (Mk. 3:14; Lk. 8:1-3).

Jesus had other followers, however, who were committed to following Him in a figurative or spiritual way but did not physically follow Him around.[4] His invitation in Lk. 9:23 is open-ended: "If anyone would come after me, he must deny himself and take up his cross daily and follow me." Not being ashamed of Him and His words was more important than going around wherever He went (Lk. 9:26). To follow Jesus came to mean openly confessed faith in Him joined with obedience

---

[2]For a full discussion of this text see T. B. Maston, *Walk as He Walked* (Nashville: Broadman Press, 1985).

[3]Michael J. Wilkins, *Following the Master* (Grand Rapids: Zondervan, 1992), 342.

[4]Ibid., 132. Wilkins cites Joseph of Arimathea and the Gadarene out of whom Jesus cast the demons as examples.

to His teachings.

First century Jews were in a good position to understand this concept of following God. The terminology of following the Lord was commonly used in the Old Testament.[5] As a covenant people, Israel was to follow the Lord and not to follow after other gods (Jg. 2:12-13). This calling meant trusting Him, worshiping Him, and obeying His laws. In the wilderness wanderings, especially with God's presence represented in the Tabernacle, there was a physical sense of following God's guidance (Ex. 40:34-38), but the concept is much broader than that. Caleb and Joshua were commended because "they followed the Lord wholeheartedly" (Num. 32:12). Likewise, Hezekiah was singled out by the chronicler as a great king of Judah because "he held fast to the Lord and did not cease to follow him" (2 Kg. 18:6). The idea of following God's example was not concretely declared until Christ came and began His ministry; but through God's covenant dealings with them and His commands to them, His people could start learning to follow.

In the Epistles the call to follow God and Jesus was issued to believers. This was a spiritual following which included emulating His example and living as He taught. Paul wrote, "Follow my example as I follow the example of Christ" (1 Cor. 11:1), and "Be imitators of God, therefore, as dearly loved children and live a life of love just as Christ loved us" (Eph. 5:1-2). Also he complimented the Thessalonians by telling them, "You became imitators of us and of the Lord" (1 Th. 1:6). They in turn became models to others (1 Th. 1:7). Peter was encouraging Christians who were facing persecution when he wrote, "To this you were called, because Christ suffered for you, leaving you an example, that you should follow in his steps" (1 Pet. 2:21). Following Jesus surely means to us that we are to seek to follow His example and live as He did. Christlikeness is our goal.

What about Imitation?

Some Christian leaders object to the idea of imitating Christ. Bonhoeffer, for instance, warned, "It is not as though we had to imitate

---

[5]Ibid., 51-69. Wilkins devotes a chapter to the way Israel's covenantal relationship was a direct prelude to Christ's call for disciples to follow Him.

Him as well as we could."[6] He was rightly cautioning against a religion of self-help. I join those who find Thomas à Kempis' book *The Imitation of Christ*[7] to be very profitable. Its motif is that by renouncing self and worldly pursuits the believer may copy Christ. Its presentation of the insidious nature of evil and the persistent temptations to which we are all vulnerable in our human weakness is both biblical and accurate. No real imitation of Jesus is possible without the power of God and without a change of heart. God, however, went to great expense to supply us with a human picture lived out in history of the righteousness which He seeks to produce in us. Loving Jesus Christ compels us to try to imitate His spirit, speech, and actions. The world desperately needs more imitators of Christ. The word in the Greek for imitate is *mimeomai*, and all Christians are called to be imitators (*mimetai*) of the Lord (1 Th. 1:6). It does not suggest mimicking in any superficial way. To be like Jesus is the height of human aspiration. It is an idealistic aim which we are to pursue depending on His grace until we die and wake up in His likeness.

Challenging Questions for Disciples

1. How would you follow Jesus' example if your unbelieving boss treated you unfairly in requiring overtime work without extra pay?
2. How would you react in a Christlike way if you were accused of saying and doing things which you did not say or do?
3. What are three ways you might humbly help another Christian that would be following Jesus' example when He washed the disciples' feet?
4. How would you follow Jesus' example of love if you were a Christian attorney defending a criminal who was actually guilty as charged?
5. How would you describe the leadership style of a pastor of a church with 300 members who was following Jesus' example?
6. What are your two weakest areas of following Jesus' model? What could you do to improve in these areas? Be specific.

---

[6]Dietrich Bonhoeffer, *The Cost of Discipleship* (New York: Macmillan, 1953), 195. I recommend reading his chapter on "The Image of Christ," 192-98.

[7]Thomas à Kempis, *The Imitation of Christ* (London: Collins Clear-Type Press, n.d.).

CHAPTER 4

GODLINESS AS A GOAL

I was living near Houston, Texas, in the early years of NASA's successful space voyages. On one occasion I heard an interview with the director of the Space Administration. He was asked, "What is the chief qualification someone needs to be selected as an astronaut?" His immediate reply was, "A strong desire to go into outer space." I had supposed he would answer, "Experience as a test pilot," or "Advanced training in aeronautics." His remark surprised me. Perhaps it shouldn't have. As intensive as the examinations and training reportedly are, a person would not endure it without that strong desire to reach the goal.

Why is it that few Christians excel in godliness? Holy living seems as remote as another planet to many believers. They are frightened or disinterested. It either seems impossible or boring to them. The New Testament clearly sets godliness as the goal God established for every saved person. That should be our objective, and is it not time we encouraged believers to have a strong desire to attain this goal? Paul's declaration to the Philippians is an illustration of the kind of desire I mean. He wrote:

> Not that I have already obtained all this, or have already been made perfect, but I press on to take hold of that for which Christ Jesus took hold of me. Brothers, I do not consider myself yet to have taken hold of it. But one thing I do: Forgetting what is behind and straining toward what is ahead, I press toward the goal to win the prize for which God has called me heavenward in Christ Jesus (Phil. 3:12-14).

Robert Browning stated, "Ah, but a man's reach should exceed his grasp or what's a heaven for?"[1] This pursuit will cause us to reach farther than we grasp, but as children of God we feel instinctively that we should be involved in this quest for godliness.

---

[1]Robert Browning, *The Oxford Dictionary of Quotations*, 2d ed. (London: Oxford, 1953), 89.

A Search for Meanings

"Godliness" is a translation of the Greek word *eusebeia* and may also be translated "piety" or "reverence." Paul used it several times in the Pastoral Epistles to refer to the whole manner of life that should come from a person being devoted to God. For instance, Timothy was exhorted with these words, "Train yourself to be godly" (1 Tim. 4:7). Obviously, not just an occasional expression of piety is called for but a consistent reverence for God demonstrated by worship and holy living.

Holiness is the very nature of God, He is transcendent. He has no affinity with sin. The New Testament use of "holiness" is based on an Old Testament foundation. As Procksch indicated, "The holiness of God the Father is everywhere presumed in the New Testament, though seldom stated."[2] The command given in Lev. 11:44, "Consecrate yourselves and be holy, because I am holy," is a priestly and prophetic theme. Israel is called to be a holy nation (Ex. 19:6), and both priests and prophets reminded the people of this calling which was to be obeyed both by ritual and practical righteousness. Ceremonial purification was intended to be joined with ethical behavior. The total life was involved. Holy days, holy places, holy garments, holy vessels, and holy oil were made holy by their association with God, the Holy One. They were object lessons in the worship of His people who were called to holiness. Holiness for the people of God also meant obeying the commands not to kill, steal, commit adultery, bear false witness, or covet.[3]

In Christianity the ritual was replaced by an emphasis on the ethical. The concept of holiness was still very important. God's demand for holiness in His people like His own holiness was still used by Christian preachers like Peter and Paul (1 Pet. 1:15; 1 Th. 4:7). It meant purity of heart and life and honesty and peacefulness in relationships. It also meant the way believers used their bodies. Paul pleaded, "Just as you used to offer the parts of your body in slavery to impurity and to ever increasing wickedness, so now offer them in slavery to righteousness leading to holiness" (Rom. 6:19). We understand that the holiness which pleases God is that which He saw in His Son when Jesus was here in human form.

Righteousness is another key word and concept in this study. God is

---

[2]Otto Procksch, "*hagios*," *TDNT*, 1:101.
[3]Ex. 20:13-17.

intent on making His people righteous. Righteousness (*dikaiosune*) means rightness or justice, especially as it concerns every phase of our relationships with others. God is the God of righteousness. The Psalmist said, "The Lord is righteous, he loves justice; upright men will see his face" (Ps. 11:7). Jesus Christ came to make God's people righteous. He said, "Unless your righteousness surpasses that of the Pharisees and teachers of the law, you will certainly not enter the kingdom of heaven" (Mt. 5:20). Paul stated, "Christ is the end of the law so that there may be righteousness for everyone who believes" (Rom. 10:4). The good news is: "God made him who knew no sin to be sin for us, so that in him we might become the righteousness of God" (2 Cor. 5:21). We must make complete righteousness our goal because that clearly is what God wants to achieve in us through Christ. Salvation from perishing was accomplished when we received Jesus and what He had done for us. Salvation from sinning is still in process when we are living for Christ who is our righteousness and holiness (1 Cor. 1:30).

To summarize what I have found in this search for meanings, godliness, holiness, and righteousness are all in the same family biblically. Different shades of meaning may be observed. Put together they describe a life of reverence and piety, consecration to God and separation from sin, and right and just relationships. They describe the example of Jesus who lived without sin and who called us to follow Him. The three words are close enough in meaning for me to feel comfortable using them interchangeably.

Reasons for Reaching

Obviously, many nominal members of churches do not take seriously the call to godliness. Few of us, even those "ordained to the ministry," give evidence of a constant vigorous attempt to achieve conspicuous righteousness. In writing about the crisis of piety, Donald G. Bloesch says, "Modern sophisticated Christians are generally scornful of piety for various reasons."[4] He mentions several reasons, such as confusion of piety with moralism, sinless perfection, or works-justification.[5] Granted that there is a lot of resistance to overcome, why should we advocate

---

[4]Donald G. Bloesch, *The Crisis of Piety*, 2d ed. (Colorado Springs: Helmers & Howard, 1988), 27.
[5]Ibid., 27-29.

reaching up for this lofty peak?

One reason is that we were **created** for godliness. We were made by God in His image to bear His likeness.[6] Since this could not mean His physical image because God is Spirit (Jn. 4:24), I take "image" to mean primarily His spiritual nature and moral character. God chose to create persons who could show the world with their lives what He is like. Sin has prevented people from achieving that perfectly except for Jesus; "He is the image of the invisible God" (Col. 1:15); "The Son is the radiance of God's glory and the exact representation of his being" (Heb. 1:3). For us, then, to become like God is to become like Jesus. This does not require a tune-up but a major over-haul, and the work must be done by God over a lifetime for those who trust in Jesus Christ and are saved by Him. Our Creator wants to do this restoration job in us and for us. Procksch said, "The aim of God is the strengthening of the heart in holiness."[7] We should desire to become holy like He is.

Second, He **commanded** us to reach for godliness. Peter restated God's command in His letter to scattered believers chosen by God "through the sanctifying work of the Spirit" (1 Pet. 1:2). He said, "Just as he who called you is holy, so be holy in all you do; for it is written: 'Be holy because I am holy'" (1 Pet. 1:15-16). Jesus commanded disciples, "Seek first his kingdom and righteousness" (Mt. 6:33). Paul exhorted Timothy, "Follow after righteousness, godliness, faith, love, patience, and meekness" (1 Tim. 6:11). Later a similar command was issued: "Flee the evil desires of youth, and pursue righteousness, faith, love, and peace, along with those who call on the Lord out of a pure heart" (2 Tim. 2:22). A disciple who intends to be obedient must strive to reach perfection, for Jesus commanded, "Be perfect, therefore, as your heavenly Father is perfect" (Mt. 5:48).

Third, this is the **purpose** for which Christ died, that we might become godly persons. One of Paul's grandest statements linking God's grace in saving us with our calling to live the Christian life says:

For the grace of God that brings salvation has appeared to all men. It teaches us to say "No" to ungodliness and worldly passions, and to live self-controlled, upright and godly lives in this present age, while

---

[6]Michael Griffiths has a good discussion of this point, *The Example of Jesus* (Downers Grove, IL: InterVarsity, 1985), 32-36.

[7]Procksch, 1:110.

we wait for the blessed hope—the glorious appearing of our great God and Savior, Jesus Christ, who gave himself for us to redeem us from all wickedness and to purify for himself a people that are his very own, eager to do what is good (Tit. 2:11-14).

The prayer of our Lord on the night before He was crucified reveals this to be one of His major concerns. He prayed for His disciples, "Sanctify [consecrate or make holy] them by the truth" (Jn. 17:17) and "For them I sanctify myself that they too may be truly sanctified" (Jn. 17:19). The Lord offered a holy sacrifice of Himself for sinners in order that we might reach for and in some measure experience the holiness of God on earth and actually become holy in heaven.

Fourth, the Scriptures teach that there is **great value** to be received from living righteous lives. A recurring emphasis in the Old Testament is that prosperity for the covenant people accompanied obedience to God and righteous living. In Moses' farewell speech he gave this instruction, "Carefully follow the terms of this covenant, so that you may prosper in everything you do" (Dt. 29:9). This is also a New Testament lesson. Contrasted with physical training or asceticism, each of which has limited value, "godliness has value for all things, holding promise for both the present life and the life to come" (1 Tim. 4:8). We are free to decide for ourselves which benefits of a holy life we value most. Paul warned that it was heresy to look on godliness as a means to financial gain, but "godliness with contentment is great gain" (1 Tim. 6:6). In my own experience inner peace and good relationships with God, others, and self are the prized values for this life which godliness produces. Remember, we are not promised the absence of opposition. In fact, Paul wrote, "everyone who wants to live a godly life in Christ Jesus will be persecuted" (2 Tim. 3:12). Nevertheless, we can be confident that no way of life is as valuable as the way of godliness, holiness, and righteousness.

A fifth reason to reach for godliness is that it is essential for **effective ministry**. The people of God must be different from the pagan culture that surrounds them. Paul exhorted Timothy, "You, man of God, flee from all this [greed and the love of money], and pursue righteousness, godliness . . ." (1 Tim. 6:11). There is no double standard. All of God's people are ministers (Eph. 4:12), and all are called to live holy lives. "Put on the new self, created to be like God in true righteousness and holiness" (Eph. 4:23). The desire to be a fruitful servant of Jesus Christ should lead a believer to pursue godliness actively. It is unlikely that a person who is not striving for wholesome holiness will be active in evangelism or in Christian service to others. How can a person proclaim holy truth and lead people in holiness without being a holy person?

The Role of the Holy Spirit

No one can travel in the way of holiness without the power of the Holy Spirit. The Spirit of God is called the Holy Spirit, both because He is Holy God and because His role is to produce holiness in a person. The holy life is supernaturally produced. The disciples are taught by Jesus to pray for the Holy Spirit: "If you then, though you are evil, know how to give good gifts to your children, how much more will your Father in heaven give the Holy Spirit to those who ask him!" (Lk. 11:13). And the Father has given the Holy Spirit to all converted believers ever since the church was born on the day of Pentecost. He promised, "You will receive the gift of the Holy Spirit" (Acts 2:38), and they did. The Book of Acts records several experiences of the Holy Spirit filling the believers and empowering them with boldness.[8] By the power of the Spirit, Christians can live godly lives in an ungodly environment. As Paul wrote, "So I say, live by the Spirit, and you will not gratify the desires of the sinful nature" (Gal. 5:16), and "You, however, are controlled not by the sinful nature but by the Spirit, if the Spirit of God lives in you" (Rom. 8:9). The Holy Spirit is the change agent who makes holy living possible. Our part is yielding to Him and actively cooperating with Him.

Let me offer you a list of eight activities which the Holy Spirit is responsible for in the life of one who is committed to Jesus Christ as Savior and Lord.

1. **He regenerates**. New birth, as Jesus taught, is the work of the Holy Spirit. The one trusting Christ is born again spiritually (Jn. 3:3-8). "He saved us through the washing of rebirth and renewal by the Holy Spirit whom he poured out on us generously through Jesus Christ our Savior" (Tit. 3:5-6). Living the new life of a Christian begins with the regeneration of the Holy Spirit.

2. **He baptizes**. Although it is listed second, I do not see this as a second work of grace. The Spirit baptism happens at conversion and new

---

[8]Acts 2:4; 4:8, 31; 6:3, 5; 7:55; 8:29; 9:17; 11:24; 13:9.

birth. I list it separately not to confuse, but hopefully to clarify. John the Baptist contrasted his baptism with that baptism which Jesus would give His followers. He said, "I baptize you with water, but He will baptize you with the Holy Spirit" (Mk. 1:8). This was later repeated by the resurrected Lord as a prelude to Pentecost when all the believers received the baptism of the Spirit (Acts 1:5, 2:4). This became the norm afterward. Paul wrote about it to the Corinthians, "For we were all baptized by one spirit into one body" (1 Cor. 12:13). If you have been saved, you were baptized by the Spirit.

3. **He leads**. Jesus, speaking about the Spirit of truth, promised His disciples, "He will guide you into all truth" (Jn. 16:13). Also, we have the promise of the Spirit's leadership in these words of Paul, "Those who are led by the Spirit of God are sons of God" (Rom. 8:14). He was speaking particularly of Christians urging them to reject the leadership of their sinful natures and to choose to follow the direction of the Holy Spirit as to where to go and not go (Acts 16:6-7). One of the reasons we can be confident of making many right decisions in our lives is because we have the leadership of the Holy Spirit.

4. **He fills**. The Holy Spirit desires to fill and control the life of the disciple, but He will not do so without our permission. Although He is already present within us, He fills most of us only occasionally, if at all. We are exhorted in the Scriptures, "Do not get drunk on wine which leads to debauchery. Instead, be filled with the Spirit" (Eph. 5:18). Instead of losing control through intoxication, we are invited to surrender control to the Holy Spirit so that He can fill us entirely. The life that He fills He uses to the glory of God. Examples are Peter, Stephen, and Barnabas.[9] The filling is not permanent and should be sought frequently. It is contingent upon surrender to the lordship of Christ. When we yield, He fills. When He fills, He uses. Praise and service are offered to Jesus from Spirit-filled persons. There is no cause for fear in one's becoming full of the Spirit.

5. **He teaches**. Jesus promised that "the Holy Spirit, whom the Father will send in my name, will teach you all things and will remind you of everything I have said to you" (Jn. 14:26). Since we believe the Holy Spirit inspired the Scriptures to be written and preserved them for our instruction in righteousness, we can feel certain that what He teaches us will be consistent with biblical revelation. An appropriate prayer to Him

---

[9]Acts 4:8-12; 6:3, 7, 55; 11:24.

is "Show me your ways, O Lord, teach me your paths; guide me in your truth and teach me, for you are God my Savior, and my hope is in you all day long" (Ps. 25:4-5).

The Holy Spirit guided the whole ministry of Jesus including His teaching, so before Jesus ascended, He assured the apostles that His teaching would continue through the Spirit.[10] For example, Peter's reception of the Gentiles came in a vision by the Holy Spirit.[11] Peter was not ready to open the door of salvation by faith to these Romans in Caesarea, but God was and He taught Peter a new lesson. The apostle responded, "I now realize how true it is that God does not show favoritism but accepts men from every nation who fear him and do what is right" (Acts 10:34). Paul was probably testifying about the same kind of experience when he wrote, "This is what we speak, not in words taught us by human wisdom but in words taught by the Spirit, expressing spiritual truths in spiritual words" (1 Cor. 2:13). Paul's teaching fills approximately half of the New Testament. He was taught by the Spirit.

6. **He empowers**. Every Christian has divine power through the Spirit for doing his part in carrying out the mission assigned by Christ. After His resurrection Jesus told His disciples, "I am going to send you what my Father has promised; but stay in the city until you have been clothed with power from on high" (Lk. 24:49). Jesus' statement recorded in Acts 1:8 clearly indicated the source of believers' power. He said, "You will receive power when the Holy Spirit comes on you; and you will be my witnesses . . ." A gigantic task of preaching and witnessing good news about repentance and forgiveness to all nations was theirs, but God's power would be given to them. The mighty deeds and proclamation of the apostles in the years after the day of Pentecost are the testimony of the fulfillment of this promise. They lived good lives, did miracles, and preached boldly through the Holy Spirit.[12]

7. **He sanctifies**. The holy God who insists that His people become holy also provides the agent for sanctification, the Holy Spirit. The Holy Spirit sets apart the saved person for Christlike living at the time of conversion. Appealing to the Corinthian Christians to live holy lives, Paul reminded them that they were "washed," "sanctified," and "justified" in the name of the Lord Jesus Christ and by the Spirit of God

---

[10]Cf. Acts 1:1-5.
[11]Acts 10:9-20, 34-38.
[12]Cf. Paul's testimony in Rom. 15:17-19.

(1 Cor. 6:11). They had been cleansed and changed, but the work of sanctification was not completed or Paul would not have been exhorting them to "flee from sexual immorality" (1 Cor. 6:18). Sanctification is a lifelong activity of the Spirit that calls for the cooperation of the believer. The Apostle wrote the above-quoted letter "to those sanctified in Christ Jesus and called to be holy" (1 Cor. 1:2). He also wrote to the Thessalonians saying, "It is God's will that you should be sanctified; that you should avoid sexual immorality . . . For God did not call us to be impure, but to live a holy life. Therefore he who rejects this instruction does not reject man but God, who gives you his Holy Spirit" (1 Th. 4:3, 7-8). We should hunger and thirst after righteousness, then, and welcome the sanctifying Spirit of holiness as He offers to fill us.

    8. **He seals**. We cannot save ourselves or keep ourselves saved. We cannot sanctify ourselves or keep ourselves sanctified. The Holy Spirit is God working in the life of the believer to separate from sin and to set apart for God's use and glory. The role of the Spirit is also to seal the believer—a work of assurance and safekeeping. Paul wrote this to the saints in Ephesus: "Having believed, you were marked in him with a seal, the promised Holy Spirit, who is a deposit guaranteeing our inheritance until the redemption of those who are God's possession—to the praise of his glory" (Eph. 1:13-14). In the first century Roman world, the Caesar or another Roman official would seal any official letter or document with wax and the imprint of his ring guaranteeing its safe delivery to the one for whom it was intended. Similarly, Christians are sealed by the Holy Spirit until God in heaven has finally received them.[13] The inner witness of the Spirit with our spirits assures us that we are God's children and heirs of an everlasting inheritance.[14]

Eschatology and Godliness

    Some may question whether our hope of heaven and eternal life with God has any motivational power for godly living in modern society. I am convinced it does. This world is still a preparation ground for the Christian. We are, each of us, on a countdown to our personal day of launch. We are bound for the promised land—a new heaven and a new earth, the Holy city. "Nothing impure will ever enter it, nor will anyone

---

[13]Cf. 2 Cor. 1:21-22.
[14]Cf. Rom. 8:16-17.

who does what is shameful or deceitful, but only those whose names are written in the Lamb's book of life" (Rev. 21:27). John also wrote,

We know that when he appears, we shall be like him, for we shall see him as he is. Everyone who has this hope in him purifies himself just as he is pure (1 Jn. 3:2-3).

In Peter's second epistle, the coming day of the Lord is described as a time when everything about the earth as we know it will be destroyed by fire. The Apostle presented this challenge: "Since everything will be destroyed in this way, what kind of people ought you to be? You ought to live holy and godly lives as you look forward to the day of God and speed its coming" (2 Pet. 3:11-12). Is this just an appeal based on fear over the world's destruction? No, there is more: "In keeping with his promise we are looking forward to a new heaven and a new earth, the home of righteousness" (2 Pet. 3:13). The hope of heaven, the expectation of the Lord's return, the destruction of the world—all of these encourage us to strive with the Spirit's aid to live godly, holy, and righteous lives now. New Testament eschatology can inspire us to make good preparation for what lies ahead.

Summary

The time is ripe for a renewal of our reach for godliness, holiness, and righteousness. Let us be people who do the best of things in the worst of times. Let us get a fresh glimpse of the glory of the holiness of God. In Jesus we see that same holiness lived in a human life in history. When we answered His call to salvation from sin, we were also called to live holy lives like His and were given the indwelling Holy Spirit to assist us. We know we have a home of righteousness, the Holy City, assured to us as an eternal dwelling place. Regardless of how many days remain for us to live on earth, let us live for Jesus. As Paul exhorted: "Since we have these promises, dear friends, let us purify ourselves from everything that contaminates body and spirit, perfecting holiness out of reverence for God" (2 Cor. 7:1).[15]

---

[15]The Greek word translated "contaminates" in the NIV is, "*molusmos*," from which we get our word "pollution."

CHAPTER 5

TRUE SPIRITUALITY

Spirituality is very prevalent among persons who live in the modern world. In spite of the near worship of science and technology and the pervasive tendency toward materialism, beliefs and spiritual practices are widespread. Not many people have quit believing that there is some truth and reality in the spiritual realm. Few are willing to conclude that biological and sensual existence in a material environment is all the life there is. The spiritual outlook may be discovered in people's fears and hopes, their feelings of guilt, their romanticism, their superstitions and traditions, as well as their religious and semi-religious practices. Few confessing atheists or total materialists can be found.

The first-century world into which Jesus came likewise was not devoid of spirituality. Many gods and goddesses were worshiped. Religions were numerous. Many ideas about humanity's origin and destiny were circulated. The primary issue was what the nature of the spiritual reality was, not whether or not it existed.

Jesus announced to one woman in Samaria what the entire world needed to hear that "God is spirit, and his worshipers must worship in spirit and in truth" (Jn. 4:24). It does make a difference what anyone believes. It always has and always will. Spirituality alone is not sufficient. That is why Jesus came "to testify to the truth" (Jn. 18:37). He said, "I am the truth" (Jn. 14:6). He lived in humanity to reveal deity. His living, dying, rising, and ascending were all revelations essential to true spirituality.

Normative Spirituality

Only Christ-centered spirituality will meet the needs of every person. One must be narrow and exclusive at that point if the Bible determines one's theology. One may grant there is some truth in all world religions and some positive results from many forms of spirituality, but there is only one Savior and Lord for the whole human family. Trust in Jesus, devotion to Him, and spiritual experience with Him constitute true spirituality.

Christians confess that they did not have any true spiritual life before they received Jesus Christ in an act of faith and surrender (Eph. 2:1-10).

True spiritual life that comes from Him continues forever. It is eternal, *aionios* (Grk.), lasting for all the ages. Once we are saved, rightly related to God through Jesus Christ, we may cultivate that relationship in many ways throughout our lives. Furthermore, the relationship is not to last "till death shall separate us," for nothing "will be able to separate us from the love of God that is in Christ Jesus our Lord" (Rom. 8:39), including death. Jesus said, "I have come that they may have life, and have it to the full" (Jn. 10:10).

True spirituality includes all that we are and do as a result of our relationship with Christ. Richard J. Hauser wrote, "Spirituality is our effort with grace to become what we have been created by our Lord to be."[1] Geoffrey Wainwright stated, "It is a praying and living in Jesus Christ."[2] Bill J. Leonard spoke of it as wholistic spirituality. He said, "Wholistic spirituality encompasses all of life, given to surprise and spontaneity, as well as to discipline and order."[3] Christian spirituality is following Jesus Christ as led by the Spirit in fellowship with the Father in order to do His will. The life of a disciple of Jesus Christ is one of true spirituality.

Needs That Are Met

One of the ways that Christian spirituality can be shown to be true is in the way the content of Christian faith meets human needs. Psychologists have helped us understand that all people have certain basic human needs beyond food, clothing and shelter. Among these are the need to be loved and to love, the need for a sense of personal worth, the need to be released from feelings of guilt, the need for hope when faced with the reality of death, and the need for meaning and purpose. While psychologists differ, and non-Christians particularly might disagree with my conclusions, I want to discuss each of these briefly and show how Jesus Christ has provided for these needs to be met.

First, every person needs **to be loved and to learn to love**. Infants'

---

[1]Richard J. Hauser, *In His Spirit* (New York: Paulist, 1982), 5.

[2]Geoffrey Wainwright, "Christian Spirituality," *Encyclopedia of Religion* (New York: Macmillan, 1987), 3:452.

[3]Bill J. Leonard, "The Spiritual Development of the Minister," *Formation for Christian Ministry*, Anne Davis and Wade Rowatt, Jr., eds., (Louisville, KY: *Review and Expositor*, 1985), 74.

primary need upon their arrival in this world is the assurance that somebody is there to care for them. You might say the first thing they need is to be cleaned up, fed, warmed and held. Yes, but in the doing of these things the caregiver may show love. Having needs met is the main way the newborn can receive love. As time goes by, the love of parents and other significant persons in the child's life may be expressed in many forms. Youth and adults of all ages require the affectionate interest and response of other persons. Also, each person needs to feel and demonstrate love for others. We were not created only to receive love but to give it as well. The severing of relationships often becomes a miserable pattern for the self-centered individual who gives no evidence of real concern for others. I placed the need to be loved first because that is how we learn to respond with love. "We love because he first loved us" (1 Jn. 4:19). Jesus Christ came to love us and to reveal how much God the Father loves us. No one who knows "the story" has grounds for doubting that he or she is loved with an everlasting, unconditional love (Jn. 3:16; Rom. 5:8; 1 Jn. 4:9-10). Moreover, Christ's call is to join with other disciples in the community of faith where love can be given and received regularly (Eph. 2:19-22; 5:1-2).

Second, everyone needs **a sense of personal worth**. We need to feel valued. Jesus was dealing with His disciples' anxiety about food and drink and clothing. They were worried and insecure. He taught them about the Father's care and His provision for the birds on a daily basis. He asked them, "Are you not much more valuable than they?" (Mt. 6:26). He proceeded to remind them that God knew about their needs and would supply them too. We are free to seek His rule and righteousness when we realize what value He has given us. Realizing that the Son of God died for us is what gives us the greatest sense of worth. As Peter replied, "He himself bore our sins in his body on the tree, so that we might die to sins and live for righteousness; by his wounds you have been healed" (1 Pet. 2:24). A person may choose to disregard the obvious value that God has placed on persons or choose to accept this sense of worth which Jesus provided by saving us at such great cost to Himself and revealing the Father's care for each of us.

Third, individuals need **release from feelings of guilt**. Of course, real guilt is a deeper problem than mere feelings, because "all have sinned, and fall short of the glory of God" (Rom. 3:23). The cross of Christ is God's remedy for human guilt. "God presented him as a sacrifice of atonement through faith in his blood," Paul wrote (Rom. 3:25).

Psychologists have discerned the detrimental effects of sustained feelings of guilt. In dealing with our guilt by offering pardon, Jesus has also made a way for us to be released from guilt feelings. The church is a fellowship of the forgiven. Our celebration in public worship includes thanksgiving for the canceling of our sin debt through Christ. "If we confess our sins, he is faithful and just and will forgive us our sins and purify us from all unrighteousness" (1 Jn. 1:9). We can be free from the burden of a sinful past and released from guilt feelings.

Fourth, all people need **hope when faced with the reality of death**. This is a world from which no one escapes alive. Through the ages, individuals have felt fear when confronted by their own death and the death of others who were important to them. In going through death for us and rising again, Jesus has enabled us to overcome this dread of death. As Paul remarked (quoting Isaiah), "Death has been swallowed up in victory" (1 Cor. 15:54) and "Thanks be to God! He gives us the victory through our Lord Jesus Christ" (1 Cor. 15:57). This liberation is also heralded in these words:

Since the children have flesh and blood, he too shared in their humanity so that by his death he might destroy him who holds the power of death—that is, the devil—and free those who all their lives were held in slavery by their fear of death (Heb. 2:14-15).

Christ is alive. He has conquered death. Through our faith in Him we are permitted to share in His victory. We have eternal life, "and so we will be with the Lord forever" (1 Th. 4:17). The resurrected Lord is our hope (1 Tim. 1:1).

Fifth, the need for **meaning and purpose in life** is universal. No other creature of God's requires it, but we do. Why do we have a life, and what are we to do with it? We have a need to know. When we accept the invitation to become a follower of Jesus, we instinctively feel we have found life's answer to those questions. We are here to worship, trust, and obey God as disciples of Jesus. Paul testified,

I eagerly expect and hope that I will in no way be ashamed, but will have sufficient courage so that now as always Christ will be exalted in my body, whether by life or by death. For to me to live is Christ and to die is gain (Phil. 1:20-21).

We believe in Jesus and serve Him along with other disciples because we believe we were created and saved for these purposes. This gives life meaning for us.

Having these five basic needs so adequately met in Christ assures us that we are on the right track. We are in a developmental process of true spirituality. God is at work in us, and He has done and is doing for us the best that could be done. Our assignment is to respond to His grace and to claim as our own what He has provided. Learning to rest on the sufficiency of Jesus, especially the consequences of His death and resurrection in our behalf, is an essential part of living the Christian life.

Balanced Spirituality

True spirituality is balanced. Again, the norm is the example of Jesus in His public ministry. He made time for solitude and also rendered service. He set aside periods for private communion with the Father and also frequently met the needs of others. He spoke to crowds and also talked to individuals and small groups. He healed physical illness and restored sinners who were hurting spiritually. He addressed immediate problems and also planned for the future. He commended the aged and blessed the children. "Well-rounded" is another way to describe Jesus in His full manhood.

Christian history reveals how easily His disciples have lost that balance. The monastic life was an attempt to recover spiritual devotion in seclusion. Hermit monks deepened their spiritual experience by withdrawal from the world. Cenobitic monks and nuns found their devotion increased in the shared life of a cloistered community. Benedictines and Franciscans tried to combine worship and work. Jesuits coupled piety with soldiering. Scholastics in the Middle Ages took a rationalistic approach to Christian faith. Christians in the East and West divided over what constitutes valid spirituality. The contemplatives and the activists have often chided each other for not being more spiritual.

Periodically, appeals for a balanced spirituality have been made. Trappist monk Thomas Merton was such a voice in this century. He described what he meant by learning to live when he said, "This means basically learning who one is, and learning what one has to offer to the contemporary world, and then learning how to make that offering valid."[4] Protestant leader Donald G. Bloesch contrasts two types of spirituality, the mystical and the evangelical, the first being more experience oriented with an emphasis on the good in persons and the immanence of God. Evangelical devotion, on the other hand, puts more emphasis on the sinfulness of persons and the need for justification through divine grace. "The orientation of evangelical piety," he wrote, "is outward."[5] Mystical religion is obviously more introspective. Elizabeth O'Connor discussed a balanced devotion to Christ in her book *Journey Inward, Journey Outward.*[6] Prayer and service belong together in one life in Christ, according to Richard J. Hauser.[7] Perhaps some leaders and some churches will make their greatest impact in one specialized area of Christian spirituality such as prayer or Bible studies or social action or healing ministry or mission endeavors, but individuals and congregations should keep striving for breadth and comprehensiveness in spirituality in order to be better examples of the whole spirituality of Jesus.

Jesus showed us the rhythm of withdrawal and return. To the mountains to pray and back to the towns to minister was a general schedule He followed. Even so, His schedule was sometimes interrupted, as ours will be, by the hurting and hungry people who demanded His help immediately (e.g. Lk. 5:16; Mt. 12:15; Mk. 2:7-13, 20). We too may have to struggle to find the quiet time, the place of prayer, or may have to push ourselves away from our study corner and prayer closet to help people face their crises and locate the Lord's power. The frantically busy person and the recluse both can profit from moving toward the center for balance in Christian spirituality.

A Word to Evangelicals

Evangelicals tend toward activism. We have highly organized churches with many meetings. The individual member is likely to feel that one is a faithful Christian if attending the main services (Sunday morning and night and Wednesday night) of the church and serving in

---

[4]Thomas Merton, *Love and Living* (New York: Bantam Book, 1985), 3.
[5]Bloesch, 96.
[6]Elizabeth O'Connor, *Journey Inward, Journey Outward* (New York: Harper & Row, 1968).
[7]Hauser, 101.

some official way such as singing in the choir, teaching a class, or functioning on a committee. Usually, a small percentage of the members are overloaded with responsibility in the organizational life of the church and may experience "burn-out" if this activity is not matched with times of personal reflection, devotional reading, and prayer. Christian spirituality includes allowing the Holy Spirit to speak to us and work in us as well as empowering us in our unselfish ministry for and with others. It is remaining in close fellowship with Jesus and also bearing fruit for Him. Worship should be both personal and corporate and should lead to words and deeds which reveal that we have been with the Lord.

If we Evangelicals have been weak in the area of private devotion, we have also been negligent, in my opinion, in our efforts to assist the poor and obtain justice for all. Some would not think of this in connection with true spirituality, but I am convinced that it belongs here. Just as there cannot be true piety without a personal pursuit of godliness in ethical living, there cannot be Christian spirituality without active compassion for the poor and disadvantaged. Jesus identified with the poor, preached to them, healed them, and fed them. He taught us that when we give food to the hungry, clothing to the ill-clad, shelter to the homeless, care to the sick, and rehabilitation to prisoners we are serving Him personally (Mt. 25:35-40). The emphasis on balanced spirituality is also made in Jas. 1:27: "Religion that God our Father accepts as pure and faultless is this: to look after orphans and widows in their distress and to keep oneself from being polluted by the world." That same Epistle contains a warning of God's judgment against the rich who hoard their wealth and underpay their workers and condemn and murder innocent men (Jas. 5:1-6). In calling for respect for the poor in the meetings of believers, the inspired writer asked, "Has not God chosen those who are poor in the eyes of the world to be rich in faith and to inherit the kingdom he promised those who love him?" (Jas. 2:5). Indeed God has consistently revealed Himself to be the friend of the poor and those being denied their rights. We should demonstrate that we are children of such a God. Inward devotion is incomplete without social compassion for the needy. Prayer was never intended to be an escape from the demands of caring for others. It is costly to care, but our loss is far greater if we fail to care. Can a person really be a disciple of our Lord without demonstrating compassion for the poor?

Summary

In a world of many conflicting ideologies and religious views, Christians need a firm grasp of normative spirituality. Only a spirituality which is centered in Jesus Christ and based on a personal relationship with Him is adequate to be the standard. The New Testament teachings are clear that true life is not found apart from following Him as led by the Spirit in fellowship with the Father.

Since persons are essentially spiritual beings, Christian spirituality proves its validity by meeting basic needs. To be loved and to learn to love, to have a sense of personal worth, to be released from feelings of guilt, to have hope in the face of death, and to have meaning and purpose in life are basic human needs met in true spirituality.

Even Christians, however, must strive to maintain balance in their spirituality so that growth inward also has an outward expression. Belief and behavior need to be united. Bible study and prayer should be combined with witnessing and service.

Particularly are we evangelicals prone to become overloaded in church meetings and activities and to be weak in our personal and private worship. Likewise, we have been weak in responding compassionately to the deprivation of the poor and victims of injustice. May God help us to be balanced in our demonstration of Christ-centered spirituality.

Study Questions

1. Can you name some non-Christian or sub-Christian forms of spirituality which are present currently in America?
2. How do these forms of spirituality fail to meet the basic needs of persons?
3. On a scale of one to ten, with one being very passive spirituality and ten being very active spirituality, where would you place yourself and most believers where you attend church?

A Prayer for Faithfulness

Teach me, Lord, I've much to learn,
  Your holy teachings to discern.
  A true disciple I would be,
To live the life you planned for me.

  Help me to follow day by day,
  And to lead others in your Way.
This is my aim, my goal, my prize,
To be found faithful in your eyes.

— *Ed Thiele*

PART TWO

GOD'S PROVISION AND OUR COOPERATION

Spiritual growth never takes place apart from the provision God makes for believers. As we are saved by grace, we must grow in grace. We do not have what it takes to lift ourselves to higher levels of holiness. But whatever God wants to see happen in us, He arranges for us to have what we need. He already knows how His plan can be accomplished before we discover it.

The Apostle Peter wrote, "His divine power has given us everything we need for life and godliness through our knowledge of him who called us by his own glory and goodness" (2 Pet. 1:3). To be fruitful disciples, to live under Jesus' lordship, to follow Jesus' example, to achieve godliness, and to embody true spirituality is really possible for us because of what God has done and offers to do for us in Christ. We all come short of the goal, but it is not because God has failed to make available what we need.

The omnipotent God has not chosen to make us all we ought to be without our cooperation. He invites us to draw near to Him. Then, He will draw near to us. He calls us to add to our lives what He supplies. Effort on our part is necessary. As Peter exhorted, "So then, dear friends, . . . make every effort to be found spotless, blameless and at peace with him" (2 Pet. 3:14).

In the five chapters that follow, we consider how we can become the fruitful disciples God desires for us to be. The focus is on the kind of heart we need and the sort of disciplines we must practice to grow spiritually. God has made it possible for us to be effective and productive, and we will find great joy in working with Him to realize those objectives.

CHAPTER 6

THE HEART OF DISCIPLESHIP

In the last sixty years (I can speak of that many from experience), the word "heart" has been prominent in American speech. We have described every emotion by reference to the heart. We have said our hearts were "broken" in sadness and "overflowing" in joy. No one's sincerity was questioned if he said something "from the bottom of his heart," nor her veracity challenged if she declared it was so "with all her heart." I am convinced that the Bible's impact on our culture has caused this use of the concept of "the heart" to be so prominent in our vocabulary.

Biblical Use and Meaning of "Heart"

A word translated "heart" is used at least 630 times in the Bible (principally, OT *leb* and *bal* and derivatives; NT *kardia*). Most of the biblical writers found its use to be essential. Only five Old Testament books and six New Testament ones have no mention of it.

Thayer's Lexicon of the Greek New Testament says "heart" denotes the seat and center of all physical and spiritual life.[1] Thoughts, feelings, desires, affections, purposes, and endeavors are said to originate in the heart. The word is used to include the whole inner life of a person. It represents the very core of one's personality.

Study of an unabridged concordance will reveal that in the Bible hearts could be broken, fixed, hardened, tender, faint, strong, pure, clean, evil, heavy, light, glad, cheerful, sorrowful, grudging, discerning, and foolish. They could be divided or undivided, circumcised or uncircumcised, deceitful, honest, troubled, sincere, lowly, opened wide, and sprinkled—and that does not exhaust the list of adjectives used to describe heart conditions.

Never do biblical writers use any of the words for "heart" to refer to the blood pump in our physical bodies. There is no reference to that part of an individual's anatomy at all. Sometimes the mind and spirit seem to be gathered up into the one term "heart."

---

[1] Joseph Henry Thayer, *A Greek-English Lexicon of the New Testament* (New York: Harper and Brothers, 1887), 325-26.

The Primacy of the Inner Life

One of the ways the Bible teaches us the primacy of the inner life of persons is by the uses of "heart." Proverbs 4:23 states, "Above all else, guard your heart, for it is the wellspring of life." A wellspring is a fountainhead or origin of a stream. It is a source of continual supply. Thus, the heart is the source of our thoughts, feelings, words, and deeds. It represents the inner life.

When Samuel was looking for God's choice among the sons of Jesse to be the coming king of Israel, he thought Eliab was his man as soon as he saw him.

But the Lord said to Samuel, "Do not consider his appearance or his height, for I have rejected him. The Lord does not look at the things man looks at. Man looks at the outward appearance, but the Lord looks at the heart" (1 Sam. 16:7).

The strong words of Israel's prophets were directed to the hearts of the hearers. While a change of conduct was demanded, the appeal was first of all for an inner response. Moral problems could never be fixed by outward alterations. "Rend your hearts and not your garments," Joel pleaded (Jl. 2:13). Multiplying sacrifices and observing holy days and reciting many prayers would never please God until hearts were right (Is. 1:10-20). After punishment from God came on the nation, prophets would explain the reason; "These people have stubborn and rebellious hearts" (Jer. 5:34). Idolatry was considered a heart problem.[2] Jeremiah wrote God's indictment of Judah, "These wicked people, who refuse to listen to my words, who follow the stubbornness of their hearts and go after other gods to serve and worship them" (Jer. 13:10). Divine judgment will be just because God knows what is inside of us—"I the Lord search the heart and examine the mind, to reward a man according to his conduct, according to what his deeds deserve" (Jer. 17:10). Motives mattered much in the message of the prophets.

Jesus also stressed the importance of the inner life. He denounced the Pharisees and teachers of the law for their misplaced emphasis on externals. They had objected to His allowing His disciples to eat without observing the traditional handwashing. He responded by quoting Isaiah,

---

[2]Ezek. 14:3-4, 7.

"These people honor me with their lips, but their hearts are far from me" (Mk. 7:6; Is. 29:13). He later addressed the whole crowd on the primacy of the inner life (Mk. 7:14-15), and then clarified the teaching for the disciples when they were alone in the house. He said "From within, out of men's hearts, come evil thoughts, sexual immorality, theft, murder, adultery, greed, malice, deceit, lewdness, envy, slander, arrogance, and folly" (Mk. 7:21-22). What an assortment of bad attitudes and actions Jesus listed which originate in the heart! By implication Jesus was offering to change people from the inside out. Repentance, faith, love, and surrender—these are the inward responses Jesus sought. These responses from us still make it possible for Jesus to reform our lives.

The Pharisees became so desperate to stop Jesus that they accused Him of driving out demons by the power of Beelzebub, the prince of demons. Jesus warned them that such talk was blasphemy since He drove demons out by the Spirit of God. Also He cautioned them that to reject the work of the Spirit is to refuse the offer of forgiveness. Then Jesus pointed out that the problem was internal, not mainly a matter of words. He said, "You brood of vipers, how can you who are evil say anything good? For out of the overflow of the heart the mouth speaks" (Mt. 12:34). Those of us who preach sermons, deliver speeches, offer public prayers, and teach lessons must be especially watchful of our hearts. Any evil stored up there will show up eventually in our words, and even careless words could be used to condemn someone on the day of judgment.

The inner life controls the outer life, even one's words. Our call from Christ to follow Him involves first of all an inward response. If we do not yield our hearts to Him, we shall never get our lives right in words and actions. The cultivation of the inner life is similar to the making of a garden. The soil we have to work with is the heart. Gordon MacDonald developed this analogy when he wrote:

Bringing order to the spiritual dimension of our private worlds is spiritual gardening. It is the careful cultivation of spiritual ground. The gardener turns up soil, pulls out unwanted growth, plans the use of the ground, plants seeds, waters and nourishes, and enjoys the harvests that result.[3]

---

[3]Gordon MacDonald, *Ordering Your Private World* (Nashville: Thomas Nelson, 1984, 1985), 118-19.

Charles H. Spurgeon is quoted as having exclaimed:

> Oh to have one's soul under heavenly cultivation, no wilderness but a garden of the Lord, walled around by grace, planted by instruction, visited by love, weeded by heavenly discipline, and guarded by divine power. One's soul thus favored is prepared to yield fruit to the glory of God.[4]

In achieving fruitful discipleship much attention must be paid to the heart, the inner life. We will think together next about ways to keep the heart right.

Ways to Keep the Heart Right

The keeping of the heart right is a lifelong process for believers. Always there are those who would make the initial work of supernatural grace so sufficient that the regular cultivation of the garden of the heart is not necessary. While I am convinced that the Scriptures teach the eternal security of genuine believers, I also believe it is the duty of true believers to keep their hearts right. Nothing more affects the nature and rate of our spiritual development than the attitudes of our hearts. The Book of Hebrews was written to exhort believers to make progress toward Christian maturity. The writer uses the history of Israel as a warning against backsliding and says:

> Today, if you hear his voice, do not harden your hearts . . . See to it, brothers, that none of you has a sinful, unbelieving heart that turns away from the living God (Heb. 3:7-12).

To harden the heart is to refuse to listen, to be unteachable. It indicates an unwillingness to submit and change. There are four steps that any Christian can take on a regular basis to prevent this hardening of the heart.

1. Love God
Jesus did not hesitate in answering the question posed by an expert in

---

[4]Cited in Corrie Ten Boom, *Clippings from My Notebook* (Thorndike, ME: Thorndike Press, 1982), 120.

the Law about which commandment is most important. He answered, "Love the Lord your God with all your heart and with all your soul and with all your mind" (Mk. 12:30).[5] Likewise, in His relation with His disciples He made it plain that love for Him was very important. Jesus said, "If you love me, you will obey what I command" (Jn. 14:15). As the anonymous hymn writer said in the hymn "O Sacred Head, Now Wounded," "Lord, let me never, never outlive my love to thee." Never stop perfecting your love for God and His Son. The heart is never right when love is lacking.

2. Pray

Speaking to God in prayer out of a felt need for His holiness is another step in keeping the heart right. David came to the Lord in prayer out of a deep sense of guilt. He prayed for mercy, for a blotting out of his transgressions, a washing away of his iniquity and a cleansing from his sin. Then he pleaded, "Create in me a pure heart, O God, and renew a steadfast spirit within me" (Ps. 51:10). Wanting to make an acceptable offering, David acknowledged, "The sacrifices of God are a broken spirit; a broken and a contrite heart, O God, you will not despise" (Ps. 51:17). One does not have to have sinned in a manner of public disgrace in order to pray fervently for a purifying of one's heart from all the experiences of falling short of the glory of God. Also, to pray for protection in temptation is valuable, asking the Lord for deliverance in advance. A good example is found in another prayer attributed to David. He said, "Search me, O God, and know my heart; test me and know my anxious thoughts. See if there is any offensive way in me, and lead me in the way everlasting" (Ps. 139:23-24). This reminds us of Jesus' teaching us to pray like this: "And lead us not into temptation, but deliver us from the evil one" (Mt. 6:13). I will have more to say later about the discipline of prayer, but here the reminder is that prayer is essential to keep the heart in good condition.

3. Meditate on the Word

Regular devotional use of the Word of God is necessary to good heart maintenance also. It seems impossible to imagine where we would be spiritually, in what desert of ignorance and despair, if it were not for the written revelation of God. God has communicated with us personally in

---

[5]Mk. 12:30 adds "and with all your strength."

the Scriptures. He warns, instructs, encourages, corrects, commands, and in other ways helps us as we open our hearts to His truth. "The precepts of the Lord are right, giving joy to the heart. The commands of the Lord are radiant, giving light to the eyes" (Ps. 19:8). A careful reading of Psalm 119 will excite any believer with new enthusiasm for Scripture, especially when considering how much more Bible we have than the psalmist had. Yet he wrote: "Blessed are they who keep his statutes, and seek him with all their heart . . . I will praise you with an upright heart as I learn your righteous laws . . . I have hidden your word in my heart that I might not sin against you" (Ps. 119:2, 7, 11). The reasons for reading God's Word are many, and more will be written later about the importance of consistent Bible reading and study. Keeping the heart right is a task that cannot be completed without reverent attention to and application of biblical revelation.

4. Live by faith

Active personal faith in God the Father and in Jesus Christ our Lord is vital to the heart's well-being. The faith we express in experiencing salvation needs to be incorporated into daily living. The grace of God that saves us initially is the grace that sustains us. As we are completely dependent on that grace for deliverance from sin and death, we are also reliant on that grace for every need. Faith is the deliberate experience of dependence and reliance on God's ability and willingness to supply our needs. Such living by faith has to be learned and developed by each disciple. Paul prayed that this might be true of the believers in Ephesus when he wrote, "I pray that out of his glorious riches he may strengthen you with power in your inner being, so that Christ may dwell in your hearts by faith" (Eph. 3:16-17). Anxiety is one of the persistent foes of such faith. The Philippians were encouraged not to be anxious about anything but to pray about everything. They were promised that "the peace of God, which transcends all understanding, will guard your hearts and your minds in Christ Jesus" (Phil. 4:7).

Similarly, Jesus comforted the disciples as His death drew near by urging them, "Do not let your hearts be troubled. Trust in God; trust also in me" (Jn. 14:1). Earlier, the Lord taught the futility of worry and the advantage of faith in the loving heavenly Father who supplies food and clothing and all we need (Mt. 6:25-34). In all four of the Gospels Jesus stressed faith. He rebuked the disciples when they showed a lack of faith. He commended men and women, Jews and Gentiles, when they demonstrated faith in Him, and He promised that even little "mustard seed" faith would accomplish wonderful results (Mt. 17:20). Moreover, the writer of Hebrews exhorted the readers: "Let us draw near to God with a sincere heart in full assurance of faith" (Heb. 10:22). Full assurance of faith comes as we learn to depend on Him in an intimate relationship.

When we regularly love God, pray, meditate on the Word, and live by faith we will keep our hearts right so that spiritual growth may continue throughout our lives. The ideal toward which we strive is to practice these steps until they become habitual.

The Temptation to Avoid Self-Examination

Looking inward is often a painful endeavor. We tend to avoid rigorous self-examination. Jeremiah delivered this warning from the Lord, "The heart is deceitful above all things and beyond cure. Who can understand it? I the Lord search the heart and examine the mind, to reward a man according to his conduct, according to what his deeds deserve" (Jer. 17:9-10). Twice in Paul's correspondence with the Corinthian church, he admonished the saints to examine themselves (1 Cor. 11:28; 2 Cor. 13:5). Surely this examination requires an investigation of the motives of our hearts. We will be tempted to ignore that responsibility while pushing ahead with our activities. Remember that Socrates said, "The unexamined life is not worth living."

Impurity and evil desire discourage introspection. We instinctively know that to confront ourselves honestly is to confront the holiness of God who lives within believers. Jesus taught that adultery is committed first in the heart that harbors lust (Mt. 5:27-28). On the other hand, our Lord said, "Blessed are the pure in heart, for they will see God" (Mt. 5:8). The more we tolerate uncleanness within, the more difficult we will find self-examination to be.

Pride and selfish ambition also get in the way of taking spiritual inventory. Humility and submission to God's authority cause us to invite correction. Knowing we cannot compete with God, however, we are apt to avoid the confrontation if governed by wholly selfish motives.

Other sins could be enumerated that harden our hearts and incline us to recoil from soul searching. What I want to emphasize is that the less our tendency is to inspect our inner life, the greater is our need to do so. Keeping the heart right is a continuous challenge and is essential to our moral and spiritual progress. God speaks in constructive criticism when we are willing to listen. Believing that He truly loves us and is trying to fashion us to be like Christ will help us to overcome the temptation to avoid self-examination.

Good and Bad Hearts for Further Study

People with Bad Hearts

1. Gehazi's greedy heart.	2 Kg. 5:19-27
2. David's lustful heart.	2 Sam. 11:2-5, 26-27
3. A couple's deceitful hearts.	Acts 5:1-11
4. A church's loveless heart.	Rev. 2:4
5. A disciple's worldly heart.	2 Tim. 4:10;
	1 Jn. 2:15-17

People with Good Hearts

1. Jesus' heart of intercession.	Lk. 13:34-35
2. Paul's heart of compassion.	Rom. 9:1-5, 10:1
3. Philip's unprejudiced heart.	Jn. 12:20-22
4. A woman's heart of adoration.	Mk. 14:3-9
5. Stephen's forgiving heart.	Acts 7:54-60

Study Questions

1. Can you describe the meaning of the term "heart" as it is used biblically?
2. Can you show from the teachings of the Old Testament prophets and of Jesus how the emphasis was placed on the inner life?
3. Are you able to recall the four steps suggested for keeping the heart right?
4. Why do you think we are often reluctant to examine our motives?

CHAPTER 7

THE DISCIPLINES OF DISCIPLESHIP

Discipleship requires disciplines to be effective. No one automatically becomes the mature Christian he or she was saved to become. As wonderful as the experience of conversion is for the believer in Jesus Christ, it does not result in immediate Christlikeness. Sometimes ministers give that impression. A verse like 2 Cor. 5:17, standing alone, sounds almost too good to be true: "Therefore, if anyone is in Christ, he is a new creation; the old has gone, the new has come!" It is an accurate description of new birth, of regeneration. It is not a prediction of instant maturity.

James S. Stewart has written a classical study of Paul and his writings entitled *A Man in Christ* in which he declares that the person in union with Christ possesses interior resources of a supernatural order which make it possible for him to live a radically different and better life.[1] Stewart was confident "Paul would have said that a Christian is a man who strives every day he lives to make more and more real and actual and visible and convincing that which he is ideally and potentially by his union with Jesus Christ."[2] He added, "To be 'in Christ' means that Christ is the redeemed man's new environment."[3] The Christian "by prayer and worship and surrender, makes contact and keeps contact with its [sic] spiritual environment, which is Christ."[4] The possession of this motive and power, however, "**does not mean the end of the Christian's striving.**"[5] One begins as a babe in Christ and "watchfulness, strenuousness, and progress"[6] are needed. Yes, in conversion a new beginning is made with glorious possibilities for growth and fruitfulness, but disciplines of discipleship must be practiced for the potential to be realized significantly.

---

[1] James S. Stewart, *A Man in Christ: The Vital Elements of St. Paul's Religion* (New York: Harper and Brothers, 1935), 193.

[2] Ibid., 199.

[3] Ibid., 197.

[4] Ibid., 198.

[5] Ibid.

[6] Ibid.

Grace and Growth

The mention of disciplines causes some evangelicals to react defensively. I could not believe more strongly that salvation is by grace alone, but growth in the Christian life is also a work of divine grace. Hear this: "But grow in the grace and knowledge of our Lord and Savior Jesus Christ" (2 Pet. 3:18); and "So then, just as you received Christ Jesus as Lord, continue to live in him, rooted and built up in him, strengthened in the faith as you were taught, and overflowing with thankfulness" (Col. 2:6-7). God's grace, His unmerited favor, rescues us from the penalty and power of sin and makes it possible for us throughout our lives to develop toward Christlikeness.

We do not get more grace by practicing the disciplines. We do not cause God to love us more by being faithful in our quest for growth. Our Father already loves us totally. Jesus has shown us once and for all the full extent of His love (Jn. 13:1). We are merely responding to that grace and love when we become obedient in doing what He wants us to do, so that He can cause growth in us. You may feel that you are not a very good Christian, as I sometimes feel about myself.[7] Nevertheless, you are just as much a child of God as any other saved believer, and He wants you and me to rest in faith while we grow to be more like His Son. We show our love for Him through trust and obedience.

Disciplines, Not Regimentation

Most disciples resist regimentation. Jesus did not behave like a drill sergeant trying to "shape up" His squad in His training of disciples. He was indeed disciplining them by instruction, commands, correction, supervised activity and motivational messages, but there is an absence of strict requirements in His training. The community of Jesus' disciples was unlike that of the Essenes, for instance, with many regulations.[8] No daily schedule was followed by Jesus and His followers. No detailed moral code was prescribed. Jesus did not try to out-Pharisee the Pharisees. Specified hours of prayer and study were not set aside for all

---

[7]Kevin A. Miller, "I Don't Feel Like a Very Good Christian." *Discipleship Journal* 47 (1988): 6-10.

[8]Michael J. Wilkins, *Following the Master* (Grand Rapids: Zondervan, 1982), 88-90. Cf. "Essenes," *Encyclopedia Judaica*, 6:899-90.

to observe. The disciples were with Jesus much of the time listening to Him teach and observing what He did and assisting Him when they could. A remarkable freedom existed among them.

Jesus did not clone disciples. Since each of them was unique, He personalized the training. Besides the teaching He gave the Twelve as a whole, He also supervised the development of each of them. Obviously, Jesus did not expect them to end up being just alike. Individuality was preserved.

In the contemporary scene disciples are going to be formed differently. Some will require more instruction than others. Their spiritual gifts will vary. All will not be leaders, but all can be useful. Jesus is still the Lord of every disciple and is committed to helping each one become disciplined and effective.

Understanding Disciplines

Disciplines are methods of gaining more knowledge of God and of ourselves and of learning to respond to God's will for our lives. They are suggested ways of receiving the spiritual power and blessings that belong uniquely to the children of God. Disciplines are essential for formation into the likeness of Christ. This involves our thought processes, our attitudes, our feelings, our words and our actions. The mind, the soul, the spirit and the body must be disciplined for the greatest spiritual growth to occur. One writer expressed his faith that "there are streams of living water into which we may place our human roots to draw the grace and strength to live and act with nobility, dignity, courage and wise, strong love."[9] The disciplines are the putting down of our human roots into the divine streams of living water.

Inward change is the primary purpose of the disciplines, and this change comes only from God. Richard J. Foster wrote, "The Disciplines allow us to place ourselves before God so that he can transform us."[10] They must be voluntarily chosen and practiced. No one can be compelled to grow spiritually. God the Father, Jesus Christ the Son, and the Holy Spirit are working together to change lives which are open and submissive. We are called to do certain things that indicate our desire for Him

---

[9]Lance Webb, *Disciplines for Life* (Nashville: The Upper Room, 1986), 32.
[10]Richard J. Foster, *The Celebration of Discipline* (San Francisco: Harper & Row, 1978), 6.

to speak to us and work in us. Dallas Willard described a spiritual discipline as "an activity undertaken to bring us into more effective cooperation with Christ and His Kingdom."[11] I would go a step further in saying that it is an attempt to grow in Christlikeness, to become more mature in Christ. Or to use Paul's words, it is an effort to become "an instrument for noble purposes, made holy, useful to the master and prepared to do any good work" (2 Tim. 2:21).

Another way of understanding the disciplines is by naming some. One should avoid saying, "These are the disciplines, and there are no others." Christian history reveals many spiritual disciplines that have been practiced and also a rich variety of them. Contemporary authors have not chosen uniformly to discuss the same disciplines. Foster has three groups of four. His inward disciplines are meditation, prayer, fasting, and study. Outward disciplines are simplicity, solitude, submission, and service. As corporate disciplines he describes confession, worship, guidance, and celebration.[12] Willard, on the other hand, while mentioning most of these, divides them between disciplines of abstinence, including frugality, chastity, secrecy, and sacrifice, and disciplines of engagement, which take in most of the outward and corporate ones which Foster discussed.[13] Another writer centers on the two basic disciplines of prayer and worship as the transforming ones and sees such practices as meditation, silence, reading, and sharing with others as accompaniments of them.[14] He shows how true perspectives, illumination, acceptance, and caring love proceed from the practice of prayer and worship.

MasterLife, by Avery T. Willis, Jr., is based on six disciplines: abiding in Christ, living in the Word, praying in faith, fellowshiping with other believers, witnessing in the world, and ministering to others.[15] Many have found this discipleship training course to be a valuable aid to a more disciplined discipleship and development of adult leadership. My own life has been greatly blessed by using its studies and activities for myself and by assisting others to engage in these disciplines.

---

[11]Dallas Willard, *The Spirit of the Disciplines* (San Francisco: Harper & Row, 1988), 20.

[12]Foster, 171 (or see his Table of Contents).

[13]Willard, 158-59.

[14]Webb, 50.

[15]Avery T. Willis, Jr., *MasterLife: Discipleship Training for Leaders* I, (Nashville: Sunday School Board of the Southern Baptist Convention, 1980), 8.

The Need for Disciplines

The busyness of American life threatens to cause dryness in our spirits. We cannot keep the motor running by depressing our accelerators without occasional refueling. The tank of Christian devotion empties out. It is not our salvation that is lost, but our vitality. We soon find we do not have any firsthand word from the Lord. We become unsure what He is really like. It is easy to be active doing good things for the wrong reasons. A fanatic is one who loses sight of his objective but doubles his speed. The pace and complexity of modern life make imperative the maintenance of spiritual disciplines.

In April of 1992 there was a bank scandal in Washington, D.C., that was publicized because members of the U.S. House of Representatives had a system whereby they could overdraw their accounts and suffer no penalties. Some congressmen had done so thousands of times. The disclosure aroused widespread indignation, probably because the freedom to withdraw more than had been deposited is a privilege every citizen who uses a bank would prefer.

Professional ministers and other Christians make the mistake also of supposing that spiritually they can keep giving out without putting in consistently. Regular deposits of inspiration and spiritual riches are essential to the effective ministry of every believer.

The believer's relationship to the Lord deserves top priority and constant attention. No relationship grows well without intimate dialogue and shared experiences. The integration of the disciple's life around Christ as its true center is a continuing need. Calvin Miller wrote, "Discipline is a matter of the inner reign of Christ."[16] Each of us must decide to put self on the cross and exalt the living Lord. The enthronement of Christ needs to be an inward act of daily devotion.

Commitment to Christian moral values is difficult to sustain in a permissive society with its steady deterioration of moral standards. An alarming diet of sex and crime and violence is constantly fed to our society by the news and entertainment media. Rarely is any ethical analysis and interpretation of current events or entertainment provided. Except for what can be done and said in the home and the church, little is offered to check the influence of low morality that is pictured as "the real world."

---

[16]Miller, *The Table of Inwardness*, 29.

In my college days at a state university I became aware that my courses in biology and psychology presented the study of human persons physically and mentally with reference to lower forms of life. A human was a vertebrate mammal with a comparatively large brain and complicated nervous system and little more than that. The only mention of "upright" was to describe vertical posture. Neurologically there was no evidence of a soul or spirit, even though the *psyche* in the Greek (from which we get psychology) meant soul. I decided then that I would never be satisfied by comparing persons downward rather than upward. As a Christian I confirmed my belief that man, male and female, was created in the image of God and was cared for by God and crowned with glory and honor.[17] Also, I promised myself that I would cultivate my spiritual relationship with my Creator and Redeemer in a daily worship time. Persons have privileges and responsibilities that none of God's other creatures will ever have. What a pity it is for people to fail to see that! How much they miss when they do not get to know the Lord and the life He has made possible for them.

Moral and spiritual victories are won by the Lord in us as we learn to practice the disciplines. Our moral and spiritual nature needs guidance and power from above. "Trust in the Lord with all your heart and lean not on your own understanding; in all your ways acknowledge him, and he will make your paths straight" (Pr. 3:5-6).

Jesus gave this instruction to His disciples, "Watch and pray so that you will not fall into temptation. The spirit is willing but the body is weak" (Mk. 14:38). This kind of watching involves vigilant use of spiritual disciplines. Temptations will continue to come; resistance to sin must arise from within us as we stay in touch with God through the Holy Spirit. Gordon MacDonald wrote, "If my private world is in order, it will be because I have determined that every day will be for me a day of growth in knowledge and wisdom."[18] Any Christian is foolish to think that repeated victory is possible in life's battles while relying on old reserves. The downward pull of the old nature, the opposition of Satan, and the attractions of a sinful world should not be underestimated.

In summary, these are three reasons why spiritual disciplines are needed: (1) the speed and complexity of modern life, (2) the importance of cultivating our relationship with the Lord, and (3) the need for moral

---

[17]Gen. 1:27; 2:7; Ps. 8:4-5.
[18]MacDonald, 87.

and spiritual guidance and power.

An Overview of Disciplines

Instead of attempting a detailed discussion of Christian disciplines at this point, I want to present an overview. My hope is that putting the spotlight on four areas of disciplines will help the reader decide on the places where his or her spiritual life needs the most help. The four areas are: (1) concentrated conversation with God, (2) comprehensive commitment to the Lord, (3) active participation in Christian community, and (4) effective ministry in Jesus' name.

Concentrated Conversation with God

Every believer wants to know the Lord better. The use of the Bible and of prayer is the most obvious way to pursue this objective. God speaks to us in His Word. The devotional use of the Scriptures involves a personal attempt to discover what God is saying to each of us about our lives. The message we receive may be one of correction, warning, encouragement, guidance, or another kind of revelation.[19] The important thing is that we reverently read and study the Bible for our own spiritual growth. Memorization of selected verses is a way to implant the Word in our minds so that we can meditate on it and use it in our conversation with the Lord.

Prayer may take many forms, but it should always be concentrated conversation with God. We may listen to God and speak to Him. Our response may be out loud or silent, written or vocal, but it should be a conscious dialogue with the Father. Usually there can be some special periods of Bible reading connected with prayer as well as intermittent expressions of relationship with the Lord such as praise, thanks, and petition during the events of a given day. Fasting may intensify our dependence on God and heighten our awareness of His presence.[20]

Comprehensive Commitment to the Lord

The disciplines of self-denial and obedience should be practiced along with our conversations with God. When He convicts us of worry, self-indulgence, pride, or other sins, we must learn to respond immediately,

---

[19]2 Tim. 3:16-17.
[20]See Foster, for an excellent treatment of this subject.

not only by confessing and forsaking the sin, but by yielding to His lordship in that matter so that positive change may occur. It is usually in connection with specific sins that we become aware of areas of our lives which have not been wholly surrendered to Him. For instance, we may feel struck with guilt over a hateful statement we have made to someone and in seeking pardon for that, may realize that we should allow the Lord to make us more loving in all of our social relationships. Also He may show us an unsurrendered area in order to lead us to a specific response. Listening to a testimony or a lesson or a sermon we may discern God calling us to obedience in our giving or serving, and the Lord may tell us what we should give to meet a particular need or how we may serve someone in his current distress. The building of Christian character comes about with the help of the Holy Spirit as we obey such commands as those regarding honesty, purity, and self-control. Learning to live under the lordship of Christ is a lifelong process, and the disciplines of self-denial and obedience will have to be practiced continually.

Active Participation in Christian Community

Our calling as disciples is into a new spiritual fellowship, a community of Christians. Disciplines like patience and forgiveness of those who mistreat us cannot be learned or practiced in isolation. For the sake of our own growth as well as for the building up of the body of Christ we have been chosen to work at maintaining loving relationships with all members of the family of God, locally and universally. This includes much more than regular attendance at church services. The response will vary some from person to person, but active participation in the church's worship, fellowship, and business are supposed to be shared by all, with consideration given to individual abilities and spiritual gifts. Why are so many members so uninvolved in the actual gatherings and activities of their churches? Nonparticipants may be the largest segment of our church populations. It may be that we have failed to teach the importance of this whole area of disciplines for the Christian. The lessons of love must first be learned in association with other caring persons. Jesus said, "By this all men will know that you are my disciples, if you love one another" (Jn. 13:35). Such love actually incorporated many disciplines as suggested by 1 Cor. 13:4-7. Dietrich Bonhoeffer's *Life Together* is a classic description of *koinonia*.[21]

Small groups within the total congregation may offer the best opportunities for learning to practice many of the disciplines. The joint support and mutual accountability provide a favorable setting for serious work on spiritual development. The sharing of ideas and feelings and experiences promotes genuine acceptance. The love and forgiveness of God are more credible among those who have received love and forgiveness from other saved sinners like themselves. However organized, small groups with spiritual objectives afford much promise in discipleship growth.

Effective Ministry in Jesus' Name

The fourth area of spiritual disciplines I want to mention is that of effective ministry in Jesus' name. The disciplines of servanthood and witnessing fall into this category. Fruitfulness generally translates into deeds of service and words of testimony and gospel presentation. Discipleship that begins and continues in conversation with God should ultimately result in unselfish, Christ-centered actions. Out of the overflow of comprehensive and progressive commitment to the Lord, a reaching out to meet the needs of others should come. One's participation in a caring community of Christians should lead to ministry inside and outside of that fellowship and declaring the good news of Jesus Christ to those who have not yet received Him by faith.[22]

The four areas of disciplines are interrelated and some disciplines may overlap areas. Balanced growth in all the disciplines and in all four of these areas is what is important.

Effective ministry does not just happen. We must get persons and needs on our hearts. We must be willing to accept training and make preparation to meet needs. We must rely upon the leadership and power of the Holy Spirit before, during, and after our attempts to minister. We must make the glorifying and honoring of Jesus our motive for ministry. This is where discipline is essential.

All four of these areas of discipline are discussed throughout the book in more detail. The purpose of this chapter was to examine the nature and place of disciplines in the believer's life. Then an overview of the disciplines was provided and the relation of these areas of disciplines to

---

[21]Dietrich Bonhoeffer, *Life Together* (New York: Harper, 1954).

[22]Delos Miles, *Evangelism and Social Ministry* (Nashville: Broadman, 1988).

each other was shown.

Study Questions

1. Can you define a spiritual discipline?
2. Are you able to state how the disciplines relate to the grace of God?
3. How many spiritual disciplines can you name?
4. Can you mention some categories of spiritual disciplines?
5. Do you feel that spiritual disciplines are essential? Why?

CHAPTER 8

PERSISTENCE IN PRAYER

My wife and I traveled from New Orleans, Louisiana, to East Africa on a short-term missionary assignment. We had calculated how many miles away from home we would be when we arrived at our destination near Nairobi, Kenya. The distance was over 10,000 miles. It was the farthest we ever had been separated from family members. We soon placed an international telephone call and with the boost of a satellite were talking to loved ones in the U.S. The reception was very clear; suddenly, we felt close to them again. How wonderful it is to stay in touch with those we cherish.

Prayer to God is like that. We tend to think of Him as far away or high up in heaven, but without the aid of communication technology we are able to converse with Him anywhere at any time. Prayer is the way He has given us of keeping in touch.

Three C's

Three words that begin with "c" help us in thinking about prayer: communication, conversation, and communion. **Communication** is the giving and receiving of messages. For each communication to occur, there must be a sender, a message, and a receiver. We are not just talking to ourselves in prayer. We are sending and receiving messages. Real communication with God is taking place.

Conversation is essentially another way of describing prayer. I am suggesting a slight distinction. Praise, for instance, may be a communication without a reply. God receives our praise, but no dialogue takes place. Adoration is reason enough for prayer. Another dimension is added when God responds to our request, and we say our prayer has been answered. Reading scriptures along with praying may allow God to speak to us first and we respond. In the exchange of meanings between persons a relationship may be developed. Our aim is an intimate relationship with the Triune of God.

Communion may occur within a relationship with or without words. My wife and I may be for several hours in the same room engaged in separate activities or reading different books without making conversation. I am aware of her presence, however, and she of mine. We do not feel lonely. We are together. At any instant, conversation could begin as needed or desired. Likewise, some of our time with God is spent like that. We are consciously living in His presence. We may be involved in study, work, or play, but we know that nothing separates us. We are in communion. At other times, of course, my wife and I are actively doing something together. Her work is mine and mine hers, or we are walking hand in hand, and there is satisfying communion that is more than words. "Enoch walked with God" (Gen. 5:24) means, at least, that communion existed between them.

Of these three styles of communication, conversation is the one we most often think of as prayer. Neither communion nor communication would be very valuable over a sustained period if there were no conversation, but the three together may enrich our fellowship with God. We are more likely to persist in prayer if we are not required to be always talking or listening.

Christian Prayer

Christian prayer is not the only form of prayer, but it is unique. Jesus encourages disciples to pray **in His name**. He is the way to the Father. Even though we are sinners, we approach a holy God on the basis of Jesus' reconciliation. Our petitions are not based on our worthiness, but His. We have boldness in approaching God's throne because of the grace He has shown us in His Son (Jn. 14:13-14; Heb. 4:14-16). We demonstrate our faith in Christ and what He has done for us by our prayers.

Moreover, Christians have the **help of the Spirit** in prayer. He lives within us to assist in several ways, not the least of which is that He guides us in praying and intercedes for us when we are unable to pray as we desire (Rom. 8:26-27). Our prayer is offered "in the Spirit" (Eph. 6:18).

Prayer is the way God **accomplishes His will** in the life of the Christian. Nothing is more important to the disciple than for God's will to be done. When growing toward maturity, we are able to discern more clearly what God's will is, but even when we do not, prayer is openness to God for Him to do whatever He pleases in us and in our situation. It is not trying to convince God to grant our will. Foster stated, "To pray is to change. Prayer is the central avenue God uses to transform us."[1]

---

[1]Foster, 30.

When we yearn to be changed into the likeness of Christ, we can be more certain of asking for what God wants to give. The beloved Apostle wrote:

> This is the confidence we have in approaching God: that if we ask anything according to his will, he hears us. And if we know that he hears us—whatever we ask—we know that we have what we asked of him (1 Jn. 5:14-15).

There are, therefore, at least three distinctive elements in Christian prayer. Christians approach God through Jesus, in His name, that is, on the basis of what He has done for us; we have the help of the Holy Spirit; and our supreme aim is for the will of God to be done.

Types of Praying

Prayer is more than asking God for something. **Petitions** are probably what comes to mind first when prayer is mentioned. People talk about getting or not getting what was asked for in prayer. The inclination is to have confidence or no confidence in prayer based on our perceived ability to get what we want from God by praying. Paul encourages us, "Present your requests to God," but even this is to be done "with thanksgiving" (Phil. 4:6). What should we ask for? Anything that we feel is important to us as disciples of Jesus and may be, as far as we know, within God's will for us.

Praise and thanksgiving are fundamental types of prayer. A valid distinction may be made between them, although they generally belong together. Praise is adoration of God because of who He is. His names, titles, and attributes are brought to mind as we praise Him. Thanksgiving focuses more on what God has said and done. We review the gifts and blessings we have received individually and collectively and express our gratitude. If there were no other reason for prayer, we should regularly praise God for His goodness, wisdom, power, love, and glory and should recount thankfully some of the many wonderful things He has said to us and done for us.

Confession is another basic type of praying. When we quit sinning, we may stop confessing. That will not happen while we live in this world, so we should continually bring to God our personal and collective admission of guilt and our request for His pardon. Peter in one early encounter with our Lord said those words which we all find difficult to say, "I am a sinful man!" (Lk. 5:13). It did not hurt his relationship with the Lord. It helped. No constant rehearsal of apology for the same sin is appropriate, however, for when we confess it, He forgives it (1 Jn. 1:9). A growing and maturing disciple will frequently be shown sins to confess, especially of attitudes and motives which were not seen before.

Commitment is another type of praying. We are invited to give ourselves to God in prayer. Submission and obedience are so vital to discipleship that surrendering should be practiced regularly. One example is Isaiah in his remarkable encounter with God. He had already confessed his uncleanness of life and had been forgiven. The Lord asked, "Whom shall I send?" (Is. 6:8). The presenting of our bodies as living sacrifices (Rom. 12:1) and the offering of ourselves to God for righteousness (Rom. 6:13) are, first of all, acts of prayer. The renewal of our commitment to the Lord is needed daily.

Intercession is a special kind of petition. While we are free to ask anything in Jesus' name that we feel is in God's intentional will, we develop in prayer when our requests are for others more than ourselves. We intercede when we put ourselves in the place of another person or group and pray what we believe they need. Paul urges us to pray "with all kinds of prayers and requests" (Eph. 6:18). Prayers for family members, for friends and associates, and for our nation, and world are intercessory. Such needs as those of the lost, sick, grieving, homeless, poor, and imprisoned call us to prayer. Also, we are specifically instructed to pray for "all those in authority" (1 Tim. 2:2), and implicitly told to pray for the boldness of all with special missionary and evangelistic responsibility (Eph. 6:19-20).

This brief discussion of types of praying is designed to help you to examine your own praying to see where attention is needed. As I have enumerated these, I have become aware of weak areas in my own recent praying. As I have written earlier, concentrated conversation with God is an essential discipline to maintain, and periodic correction and expansion are profitable. The use of a prayer journal whereby we pray intentionally for selected categories of persons on certain days of the week will likely broaden the scope of our intercession. Employment of an aid like a missionary prayer calendar may also be beneficial.

Ways Not to Pray

As important as prayer is to our discipleship, none of us wants to do it wrongly. Jesus taught two bad ways to pray. The first is to pray **proudly**. The prayer practices of the Pharisees were an illustration of this. Piety for public display may gain one a reputation for religiosity but wins no approval from God (Mt. 6:5-6). Likewise, prayer that is self-congratulatory and prejudicial never pleases the Father. "For everyone who exalts himself will be humbled, and he who humbles himself will be exalted" (Lk. 18:14). Pride has no place in the prayers of believers.

Another mistake Jesus taught us to avoid is praying too **wordily**. God is not impressed by fluency. Pagans can babble. "They think they will be heard because of their many words" (Mt. 6:7). We are not supplying God with information when we pray, nor are we trying to overcome His reluctance to answer us by the persuasiveness of our speech. This may induce the elimination of trite phrases that have no real meaning for us, too. Sincerity and succinctness are more necessary than much speaking. God knows our needs and our hearts and He wants simplicity in our prayers.

A Pattern of Prayer

According to Luke's account, Jesus was responding to the disciples' request, "Teach us to pray" (Lk. 11:1), when He gave them a pattern. The longer form of the model is in Mt. 6:9-13. I do not see any harm in praying it as given, but it probably was not intended for that purpose. The greater value lies in accepting it as a guide for our praying. An extensive exegesis of the passage is not attempted, but a few observations about the pattern are furnished next.

The pattern has four concepts pertaining to our relationship with God and four that are more directed toward our own needs.[2]

The first four are:
1. Seeking intimacy with God by approaching Him as our Father
2. Sanctifying and praising His name because He is holy
3. Seeking His kingly rule over all people and all things

---

[2]Most commentators see only six petitions here with a double-pronged statement in the third and sixth.

4. Surrendering to His will right now on earth starting in us.

And the other four are:
1. Asking for our daily needs to be supplied
2. Asking for forgiveness of sins committed
3. Asking for guidance away from testings
4. Asking for deliverance from evil and Satan.

The model begins with the acknowledgment of Father God who is high and holy, and concerned about our seeking His kingdom and following His plan. It continues with admission of our dependence, sinfulness, and vulnerability and with our confidence in His providence, forgiveness, guidance, and salvation. One does not have to include all of these matters in each prayer and is not discouraged from praying about other things. The pattern, nevertheless, offers us some direction from our Lord for our praying.

Persistence in Prayer

Jesus taught persistence in prayer. He told His disciples a parable (Lk. 18:2-5) to show them that they should always pray and not give up (Lk. 18:1). "A judge who neither feared God nor cared about men" granted justice to a widow in her appeal because he saw how she persevered. God is very unlike that bad judge except that He does anticipate continuance in prayer. Those who really trust Him will keep coming before Him in prayer, and He will answer the requests of "his chosen ones."[3]

Does persistence in prayer mean that we will keep begging for something we want until we get it? I do not think Jesus intended to teach that. We are not trying to persuade God to change His mind and give what we ask because we are a nuisance to Him. Rather, He was saying that we should be tenacious about praying even when we do not see immediate results. As long as a problem or need exists, we should continue to ask God to meet it. We must not have a fainthearted faith.

Until God answers "yes" or "no" to our petition or intercession, we do right to persist. He may be saying "Wait" so that we may derive the blessings of earnest and prolonged prayer. I remember seeing a husband

---

[3]Cf. Lk. 11:5-10.

saved whose wife had prayed for his salvation and asked others to do so for at least twenty years. During those years of intercession she had been an inspiration to many Christian friends. She never gave up.

George Muller began in 1844 to pray daily for five persons to be converted. It was eighteen months before the first was saved and five years before the second came to Christ. Six more years elapsed before the third was won. Of the other two, one became a Christian before Muller's death and the last a few years after he died.[4] Although the Bethesda Orphanages in England are what he is best remembered for, perhaps his greatest work was prayer. He trusted God to supply every need, his own and the children's. He was eager to show what can be accomplished by faith alone so that God's glory might be seen by everyone.

"Pray continually," Paul wrote (1 Th. 5:17). This should be the disciple's ambition, to have regular times of prayer and to pray in different ways in between those scheduled times so that we are in constant fellowship with God.

Freshness through Variety

God is not boring, and prayer to Him should not be dull either. We are given gifts of imagination and creativity that can be used to make prayer more exciting for ourselves and for others with whom we pray. Remember that God planned variety for every aspect of His creation. He likes it when we use variety to maintain freshness in our relationship with Him. This is another way of returning to Him what He has given to us. Let me suggest some means of maintaining a dynamic prayer life.

Meditation on prayers recorded in the Bible can be stimulating. The Psalms are full of prayers. All kinds of life experiences were occasions of prayer for David and other writers. Although they were set to music for wider use, many of them seem to have been genuine prayers first, heart cries in times of trouble, and love songs to God in periods of personal devotion. Very often one of them will resonate with your own spirit so that you can make the psalm your own prayer. Great biblical prayers like Solomon's at the dedication of the temple (1 Kg. 8:22-54) deserve frequent reading and reflection.

---

[4]Roger Steer, *George Muller: Delighted in God* (London: Hodder & Stoughton, 1975), 267.

The **published prayers of other believers** may also be used to refresh your spirit. Check with your religious library or book store for suggestions. Many excellent religious poems are written as prayers and you are free to borrow their inspiration for your own prayer fellowship. A lady complimented her pastor by saying, "Pastor, you have taught us to pray about things I did not realize God was even interested in." A similar reaction may be yours as you read the prayers of others.

Music was meant for prayer and prayer for music. Both may be rightly called "the language of the soul." **Your hymnal** can be a gold mine for your devotional life. A true hymn is addressed to God and not intended to be performed but prayed. Do not think just of religious songs about prayer like "Sweet Hour of Prayer." Instead select those like "O Master, Let Me Walk with Thee," "My Jesus, I Love Thee," "Have Thine Own Way"—such beautiful prayers! Your ability to sing them is not essential. A reverent reading will suffice. If you choose to sing them, sing to the Lord.

Writing out prayers can also strengthen your personal worship time. One has to concentrate and sort out one's feelings in order to find the words that fit. Any ruts that are forming in our prayers become exposed through the discipline of writing. Surely God deserves honest and carefully worded prayers as well as poured out feelings. Biblical prayers like those in the Psalms, which give evidence of both the Holy Spirit's inspiration and the author's excellent construction, should free us to try writing some of our own prayers.[5] Pray some of the time with your pen or computer.

Selecting a **prayer partner** or meeting occasionally with a group for prayer can add vitality to your praying. Jesus recommended both privacy in prayer (Mt. 6:6) and uniting with a few others in prayer (Mt. 18:19-20). We learn from those with whom we pray, our feelings are intensified by theirs, and our faith is fortified by theirs. I have learned to be more natural in prayer from prayer partners. I remember one friend who often laughed with God when we prayed. Because I had never thought of doing so, his freedom helped me to be more joyful in some prayer experiences. Another would make a request of the Lord and immediately thank Him for granting it. That is showing confidence of asking according to His will. Openness to learn from others is valuable in

---

[5]As an example of a carefully constructed prayer, Psalm 119 is an acrostic poem. The verses of each stanza begin with the same letter of the Hebrew alphabet.

prayer as well as in other phases of discipleship.

Also, the way we use our bodies can enhance our prayers. **Kneeling** has been since ancient times a way of showing respect for one with greater authority. The Psalmist wrote, "Come, let us bow down in worship, let us kneel before the Lord our Maker" (Ps. 95:6). Even **prostrating ourselves** on the floor may be an aid in times of anguish such as deep intercession, like Moses and Aaron falling face down before God to cry out in behalf of Israel (Num. 16:22). Ezekiel often stretched out himself on the ground in awe of God's revealed glory (Ezek. 1:28; 3:23; 43:3; 44:4). Of course, **standing** in the presence of another is also a way of showing honor, hence, standing is suitable for praising God. In the revival of Nehemiah's day, the Levites called out to the Israelites and said, "Stand up and praise the Lord your God, who is from everlasting to everlasting" (Neh. 9:5). Also, hands are very expressive of feelings. **Raising the hands** while we pray can accompany our plea for help as in Ps. 88:9 and 141:2. If it is disruptive in public worship, it may still be practiced when praying alone. **Walking or jogging** while we converse with God may also open our eyes to beauty and blessings for which we have not previously expressed thanks. I encourage you to use your body to bring diversity to your prayers.

So much time is spent working or traveling to and from work, it seems essential that we learn to **pray while we do other things**. Some types of driving, as with cruise control on an interstate highway, and some types of work, like stuffing envelopes, lend themselves to prayer. Brother Lawrence was noted for praying in the monastery kitchen while he worked among the pots and pans. Frank Laubach, missionary to millions, urged Christians to learn to pray "flash prayers." That means praying on the spot as you see a person or think of him or her or as you hear an ambulance siren or a bird's song. Waiting times in doctor's offices and at checkout counters can be profitable interludes of prayer. Prayer combines nicely with other events, and remember, prayer is also conscious awareness of God's presence when we are not forming ideas to communicate.

No disciple will grow spiritually beyond his or her custom of prayer. Christ is the Source of our fruitfulness. Our union with Him makes fruitfulness possible. Deliberate abiding (residing, remaining) in Him makes the bearing of much fruit possible. Persistence in prayer is essential to our fruit production. It is not what we know about prayer but how we pray that matters.

Study Questions

1. How would you distinguish between communion, conversation, and communication in prayer?
2. Can you name three ways Christian prayer is distinctive?
3. What type of praying do you feel needs the most attention in your own life?
4. What special value do you find in the Model Prayer Jesus gave us?
5. Have you found one or more ways to add freshness to your prayer experiences?

CHAPTER 9

CONTINUAL USE OF THE SCRIPTURES

We are a people of the Book. There would be no Christians in the world today were it not for the Bible. We do not worship the Bible, but we do worship the God who has revealed Himself in the Bible. Even though the fullness of God's revelation is in Jesus Christ, we are dependent on the inspired Scriptures for our knowledge of Jesus. Jesus does not derive His authority from the Scriptures, but they bear true witness to His authority. We have come to know Him who is Savior and Lord because the Bible was written and preserved and translated so that we could accept Him and its message about Him by faith. As we came to faith by the use of Scriptures, we are nurtured in the faith by them, that is, provided that we continue to use them.

Disciples Are Learners

Lifelong learning about Jesus Christ and the Christian life are necessary. Because the Old Testament was the Bible He used and contains the prophecies which He fulfilled, it is precious to us. The New Testament is not more inspired, but it is more cherished by us because it is all about Him. We believe in the unity of the Scriptures as the revelation of the one God who wants us to know Him and the truths He has disclosed to us.

In a Roman Catholic funeral service that I attended, I saw the priest, before and after reading the gospel, lift the printed copy of the Scriptures to his lips and kiss it. Later I attended a Bar Mitzvah inducting a thirteen-year-old boy into a new period of religious responsibility at a Jewish synagogue. The rabbi took the sacred scroll of the Torah from its rack and kissed it, then proceeded up one aisle and down the other kissing it enthusiastically. Both times I was surprised and convicted. I wondered, since I had never done this, if it were obvious to others that I really do love the Word of God. Do we treat every copy of the Scriptures respectfully and do we feel affection for the revelation God has given us? We probably will choose other ways to exhibit it, but we should openly cherish His recorded Word.

We who frequently handle copies of the Scriptures need to be reminded of their holiness. Paul in his second letter to Timothy reminded him that from infancy he had "known the holy Scriptures" (2 Tim. 3:15). We use similar language and also speak of "the Holy Bible." Why? Because it contains the words of a Holy God written down and preserved by Holy Spirit directed men who were set apart for service to God. Peter wrote:

> Above all, you must understand that no prophecy of Scripture came about by the prophet's own interpretation. For prophecy never had its origin in the will of man, but men spoke from God as they were carried along by the Holy Spirit (2 Pet. 1:20-21).

Also, the Bible is holy in its purpose to save and sanctify sinners. The Scriptures had made Timothy "wise for salvation through faith in Jesus" (2 Tim. 3:15). Jesus prayed for His disciples, "Sanctify them by the truth; your word is truth" (Jn. 17:17). Essential to the continuing sanctification of every believer is the sustained use of the Bible.

Values of Bible Reading and Study

A part of the Christian's value-system should be certainty about the values of Bible reading and study. It is not hard to come up with excellent reasons for practicing this discipline. Periodic review of our spiritual needs will lead us along the right path. Let me briefly discuss seven values of consistent use of the Scriptures.

Knowledge of God is the first of these values. There is no comparable way of learning the truth about God. General revelation is of some value (Rom. 1:20), but no one has ever received enough knowledge of God from observing His creation to be saved or to grow in godliness. Historical revelation provides clues to the nature of God, but without a key to interpret history from the divine perspective, few dependable conclusions can be drawn. To know God we must have a message from God, a personal revelation. God has wanted to be known by humanity so much that He has sent His Son; and to those who trust Him, He has given His Spirit to lead them into all truth (Jn. 16:13). The Scriptures are God's gift to us so that we may know what He has done and what He is like and may respond in spirit and truth. Through the inspired writers we are able to interpret historical events as records of God's activity. Furthermore, the Bible presents the gospel of Jesus Christ as the apex of God's self-revelation. One who desires to know God will not ignore the Bible but will read and study it regularly.

The second value of Bible reading and study is **understanding ourselves**. The modern person is a complex creature. Our scientific and technological information is extensive, but we continue to reveal an inadequate awareness of our own nature and destiny. To the extent that any person will seek the truths about persons revealed in the Bible, however, an increasing understanding of human beings will be acquired. One can learn how gloriously one was created, how susceptible to sin one has become, what moral and social responsibility one carries, and what salvation and hope one needs. All that one requires for effective living and eternal life has been provided by God and may be learned through the study of His Word.

Developing faith is a third value derived from persistent Bible reading. "Without faith it is impossible to please God, because anyone who comes to him must believe that he exists and that he rewards those who earnestly seek him" (Heb. 11:6). The Bible records the successes and failures of those who were trying to exercise faith in God and those who refused to do so. Stories about real people like ourselves are recorded so that we can be encouraged and warned by the decisions they made. Best of all, the Scriptures feature the work of God the Father, Son, and Holy Spirit so that our confidence in Him can grow. The exhortation, "Build yourselves up in your most holy faith" (Jude 20), calls for a response of continued reading and study of the Bible.

Another value is that of **strengthening character**. This includes the ability to say "no" to temptations to sin. Jesus used His knowledge of the Scriptures in conflict with Satan and lived without sin. To be prepared for our spiritual warfare, surely we need a thorough comprehension of biblical truth. "Take the helmet of salvation and the sword of the Spirit, which is the word of God," Paul wrote (Eph. 6:17). A positive program of regular Bible reading fortifies the child of God for right choices. Deep convictions regarding revealed truth are imperative for strong Christian character. Consistent use of the Scriptures, like regular use of a muscle, is what produces strength.

Fifth, **deriving inspiration** is a value of Bible reading and study. It is not enough to know the correct thing to do, one must be inspired to do it. Praise and gratitude to God are evoked by our encounters with Scriptures. Reminders of what God has done for us, references to His attributes, and recollections of His promises comprise much of the biblical material. A common occurrence for a Christian should be to close a quiet time in the Word with an enthusiastic resolve to live for the Lord more confidently and courageously. The Bible is inspired and it is inspirational. The Lord's message to Joshua after the death of Moses is a good example.

> Be strong and courageous, because you will lead these people to inherit the land I swore to their forefathers to give them. Be strong and very courageous. Be careful to obey all the law my servant Moses gave you; do not turn from it to the right or to the left, that you may be successful wherever you go. Do not let this Book of the law depart from your mouth; meditate on it day and night, so that you may be careful to do everything written in it. Then you will be prosperous and successful. Have I not commanded you? Be strong and courageous. Do not be terrified; do not be discouraged, for the Lord your God will be with you wherever you go (Jos. 1:6-9).

Of course, God's view of success and prosperity is different from the secular person's view; but the promise of blessings is significant, however stated. The Bible is full of inspirational treasures.

Another reason to value sustained use of the Scriptures is **receiving guidance**. How was Moses able to guide the Hebrews through the forty years of journeying through the wilderness? God guided him. The words of God especially led him so that he could lead the people. Unlike Moses, we have in the Scriptures, a wonderful resource from which to obtain answers. Perseverance in reading and patience in studying the Bible will show us the principles that will help us make wise choices and discern God's will on many issues we face. Also, the Lord may use specific Scriptures to direct us in important decisions. We are prepared to accept both general and specific guidance when we are consistently reading our Bibles.

Preparation for serving others is a seventh value of Bible reading and study. We need to attain such familiarity with the Scriptures that we are able to assist others with their spiritual problems. A person disturbed by lostness can be helped best by a friend who knows, not only the Christ who saves, but the biblical truths of how He saves and on what conditions. To be His messengers we must be well acquainted with His message. Furthermore, many Christians have difficulties for which they need counsel, and believers with a good grasp of God's Word may be equipped to serve them. We have this urgent charge, "Preach the word;

be prepared in season and out of season; correct, rebuke, and encourage with great patience and careful instruction" (2 Tim. 4:2). Also, this confidence is expressed: "All Scripture is God-breathed and is useful for teaching, rebuking, correcting and training in righteousness, so that the man of God may be thoroughly equipped for every good work" (2 Tim. 3:16-17). What an advantage the student of the Scriptures has in readiness to minister to others!

Do you have any doubt about the values of using the Scriptures consistently? Let me suggest that you review the seven values I mentioned. If you are not convinced of one or more of these, would you be willing to test your doubt by recording daily what you experience from Bible reading and study over a month's time? Perhaps you would even testify to others about the results.

Simple Steps in Using the Word

The way we approach the Word of God is very important. It is different from every other book we handle. We should open it prayerfully, trying to find what God is saying to us and asking Him to reveal truth to us as we read and study it. The spirit of young Samuel after being coached by the old priest Eli is seen in his prayer, "Speak, for your servant is listening" (1 Sam. 3:10). That is the spirit most appropriate for devotional reading of the Scriptures. Continue your study in that attitude of humble prayer. Expect God to speak to you.

Do your best to understand what the biblical passage you are reading meant to those who first read it. It is difficult to seize the correct meaning for ourselves now until we have accurately interpreted its meaning for those who first received it. Use your imagination and any background information you possess to put yourself into the historical setting as much as possible. I will write some suggestions later about tools that can help us do this.

Whenever possible use pen and paper to write down what God is saying to you as you use the Bible. Most of us can think better and recall longer what we have committed to paper. I think better when I am preserving visually what my heart is hearing. Full sentences are not necessary. Key words may be sufficient clues to review the insights received. A paraphrase or a summary of a passage or an entire chapter is often valuable. Writing down your thoughts and impressions enables you to concentrate on the communication being received.

Another simple step is to plan to act in response to God's message to you. James said, "Do not merely listen to the word, and so deceive yourselves. Do what it says" (Jas. 1:22). If you receive a warning, heed it. If you receive a promise, claim it. If you are rebuked for a sin, confess it. If a correction is given, make the needed change. If a command is issued, obey it. If God's glory is seen, praise Him. If a lesson is imparted, learn it and teach it to someone else. The Bible aims to remake us into the likeness of Christ. Let's allow these marvelous words of holy Scripture to have a major impact on what we are and what we do. Jesus warned, "Not everyone who says to me, 'Lord, Lord', will enter the kingdom of heaven, but only he who does the will of my Father who is in heaven" (Mt. 7:21). His will is revealed in His Word.

Bible Reading

Systematic daily reading of the Bible is a challenging discipline which every disciple should practice. If that sounds too dogmatic to you, let me assure you that it is my firm conviction and is based on a lifetime of experience. I do not mean to say that I have never missed a day of reading God's Word, but the pattern has been set for so long that it is hardly possible for me to miss a day without being painfully aware of it. I encourage you to make the practice habitual and do it not grudgingly but cheerfully. Cultivate the affection for the whole Bible that the Psalmist expressed for the Law when he wrote, "The law from your mouth is more precious to me than thousands of pieces of silver and gold" (Ps. 119:72).

Certain sections of the Scriptures are more compelling than others for us. The Gospels are the most popular, reasonably so. Acts and the Epistles come next. Reading the New Testament through at least twice a year is easily accomplished. It contains 260 chapters, so one and a half chapters per day would accomplish this. The Psalms number 150; many are quite short. Reading one a day, a person can cover them all in five months. While I do not recommend reading the Bible straight through because of the difficulty of sustaining interest in some parts like Leviticus, the entire Bible can be read in seventy-one hours or less.

It is wise to have a scheduled time for reading the Bible, preferably in the first part of the day, and to have a plan for your reading. For instance, three chapters a day and five on Sundays will take you through the Bible in a year. Combining two chapters in the Old Testament with one in the New is a conservative daily schedule. If you want to follow a printed plan, *Open Windows*[1] and other devotional guides are available with suggested daily readings.

Another recommendation is that you read with the purpose of receiving a message from God. It may be found in one verse or even in one word that you read. Think about it and relate it to what is going on in your life. Absorb it so that it becomes a part of you and so that you can share the impression with someone else if the opportunity arises. Writing it down will reinforce its power in your heart. What John wrote in the prologue of Revelation is applicable to all Bible reading; "Blessed is the one who reads the words of this prophecy, and blessed are those who hear it and take to heart what is written in it, because the time is near" (Rev. 1:3).

Methods of Bible Study

Bible study is different in that more intense concentration is maintained on all aspects of the Bible passage being considered at any given time. Usually, notes are taken and some organization of the ideas discovered is attempted. The purposes for Bible study may differ, but I am focusing on the discipleship aims of attempting to grow toward Christian maturity and to help others in their growth.

One method of study I will call the **book** method. The aim is to gain an extensive knowledge of one book in the Bible. First, that book is read repeatedly. It may be outlined so that its prominent features and main divisions can be clearly seen. Often one theme can be found. Whenever possible the probable author, recipients, purpose, and date of the book are decided, and the circumstances surrounding the writing are determined. The study may be concluded by arriving at its special relevancy for our time.

Another method may be named the **type of literature** method. The books of the law, for instance, may be studied as a unit. Different groups in the Old Testament might be studied separately, such as the books of history, the major and minor prophets, the poetry and wisdom literature. Biblical history is of a special type. Hebrew poetry is unique. A grasp of the characteristics of each literary classification can aid the interpreter

---

[1]*Open Windows* is published quarterly by The Sunday School Board of the Southern Baptist Convention, 127 Ninth Avenue, North, Nashville, TN 37234.

immeasurably. In the New Testament a study of the Gospels would be fruitful—observing them as a type of literature, not history or biography. Within the Gospels, the parables are an interesting study. They are a special kind of literature and keys to accurate interpretation may be learned. Since our Lord was so fond of using parables, we should learn to appreciate them too. Every Bible student needs to take into account the kind of literature he is examining.

A third method is **topical**. The study of a topic like poverty would cause one to investigate how the Law said the poor should be treated, how different kings of Israel and Judah treated the poor, how the prophets defended the poor and attacked the rich who exploited them, and what proverbs applied to the life situation of the poor. Then, of course, Jesus' attitude toward the poor, and His and the churches' actions to assist the poor, would be scrutinized. The rest of the New Testament would be searched for further lessons about poverty. An unabridged concordance would be useful in seeking biblical references which contain the key words regarding poverty such as poor, needy, orphans, widows and aliens. A topical method may also be thematic, pursuing a theme like "God's Regard for the Poor."

Doctrinal Bible study is another method. Somewhat topical, the procedure is different. The student is bent on locating all the Scriptures which shed light on a particular teaching of Christianity. The doctrine of salvation could be examined and the contrast between the Old Testament understanding of deliverance from death, defeat, or disease, and the New Testament concept of salvation from sin, spiritual death, and hell could be observed. More than word study is involved. *The Disciple's Study Bible* has been published to provide assistance in studying twenty-seven major doctrines.[2] By its composition it suggests that outlining, summarizing, compiling all biblical references and comparing each reference with others on the same doctrine are valuable techniques. No doctrinal view should be considered complete without an examination of every pertinent biblical reference.

The **biographical** method is another interesting way to study the Scriptures. The Bible describes many intriguing characters. Genesis, Romans, Galatians and Hebrews all contain information about Abraham, for instance, and he is mentioned in twenty-three other Bible books. Should not Christians become familiar with biblical persons who served

---

[2]*Disciple's Study Bible*, New International Version (Nashville: Holman, 1988).

God conspicuously in their times? The only reliable resource we have is the Bible, and even a Bible dictionary while supplying other profitable data will chiefly draw together what the Bible contains. An investigation of relative unknowns like Epaphroditus and Silas offers lessons on discipleship.

One final way I want to discuss briefly is the **personal characteristics** study. As disciples seeking to mature in likeness to Christ, we are wise if we identify our weaknesses and acquire enlightenment from the Scriptures concerning the desirable characteristics in which we are deficient. For example, suppose you wanted to study patience. Patience is a quality lacking in many people. It is a quality every Christian needs while waiting for the fulfillment of God's promises (Heb. 10:36). Job is an example of patience, as is any good farmer; readiness for the Lord's return requires it (Jas. 5:7-8). Galatians 5:22 includes patience as a fruit of the Spirit. That is how you would get started on the study of a personal characteristic. The use of an unabridged concordance would greatly facilitate your efforts.

Tools for Study

So many tools are now available for Bible study that I am hesitant to discuss the subject, particularly since programs for personal computers can be purchased to do much of what I have depended on books to do. I will be brief. My aim is to help the beginner, so the advanced Bible student will likely want to skip this section.

A good Bible dictionary is essential. It provides so much useful background information and synthesizes biblical data to make it readily available. For instance, one could learn more about Solomon's temple quickly from a dictionary entry than from Scripture reading alone. A drawing or a picture of a model as well as a summary of biblical information in outline form would probably be supplied.

An unabridged concordance is also necessary. Most study Bibles contain a limited concordance which often frustrates the student by not including the very reference one is seeking. Satisfaction comes from having examined every Scripture where a certain word is found. An analytical concordance will also distinguish between the different Hebrew and Greek words which carry the same or a similar meaning. These distinctions are discernible even by a person who has not studied the biblical languages.

Books for word study are also useful. Some are word study books of particular portions of the Scriptures and some are dictionaries of Old Testament and New Testament words. A scholar or team of scholars has prepared a thorough discussion of each word listed and may include the historical background as well as biblical usage. Grammatical factors which affect the translation are also pointed out. Although some lexicons require knowledge of the Hebrew or Greek, others do not. Several Bible translations will also aid the student.

In addition, a one-volume commentary or a set of commentaries will be beneficial. Choose carefully. Seek the advice of others. The theological position of the commentator is a factor to consider in making your selection. You would expect to find historical and critical information about each Bible book, chapter and paragraph summaries, and verse by verse comments. Do not rely on the commentary to do your study for you, but let it guide and supplement your own efforts to arrive at the best interpretation. Every believer has the right and responsibility to interpret the Word of God for himself or herself.

Also, some excellent books are available on how to study the Bible. An atlas of Bible lands will provide additional maps and geographical details. A book on Bible history will enable you to put the pieces of the story together in proper sequence. Daily life at different periods in Bible times is described in books that draw upon archaeological discoveries and extra-biblical historical documents. Numerous tools are available to help you dig deeply in the holy Scriptures.

Memorization

How glad I am that soon after beginning my journey as a Christian, I was encouraged to memorize Bible verses. A set of twelve Bible verses printed on handy little cards got me started. Also a Christian friend and I encouraged each other by quoting verses with the reference "fore and aft" while we walked to high school and back. It was not just an intellectual exercise. I never did anything more practical. For instance, 1 Cor. 10:13 is one of the first verses I committed to memory. It says, "There hath no temptation taken you but such as is common to man: but God is faithful, who will not suffer you to be tempted above that ye are able; but will with the temptation also make a way to escape that ye may be able to bear it" (KJV). Even though I like a modern translation better, I quoted it here as I first learned it. I have *used* that verse thousands of times since getting it programmed into my memory bank. Temptations came frequently; although I sometimes failed to overcome them, God has been faithful.

Verses of assurance like Jn. 5:24, Bible promises like Phil. 4:13, warnings like Lk. 12:15, commitment verses like Lk. 14:33, witnessing words like Rom. 10:9-10, 13 and many others deserve to become woven into the fabric of our lives. Memorization makes them ours in a special way. Although several memory systems are available, you may prefer to develop your own. Some sort of plan or system will give you a track to run on.

Let me offer you a few suggestions.

1. Start slowly; memorize just one to four verses a week if you are a beginner.
2. Write the verses on cards small enough to carry easily in your pocket or purse and later file conveniently.
3. Memorize accurately and learn the reference.
4. Utilize different methods of memorization that fit your style, such as tape recording, visualization, repeating aloud, and drilling with a friend or family member.
5. Review frequently until each verse is grooved into your brain. This may require six weeks of almost daily repetition and weekly repetition thereafter.
6. Use time spent waiting in various places to work on memorization. When appropriate, give your cards to another individual to be checked. That person will receive a blessing.
7. You will find the verses you memorize are ideal for meditation, inspiration, fortification, conversation, proclamation, and prayer.

Remember, "you have been born again, not of perishable seed, but of imperishable, through the living and enduring word of God" (1 Pet. 1:23). Therefore, "Like newborn babies, crave pure spiritual milk, so that by it you may grow up in your salvation, now that you have tasted that the Lord is good" (1 Pet. 2:2-3). If spiritual pride is a problem for you, try memorizing Lk. 14:11, but keep storing up God's truth in your heart as long as you live.

Study Questions

1. How can you show affection for the Bible as God's Word to you?
2. If you were recommending Bible reading and study to another Christian, to what values would you point?
3. Can you name four simple steps in the best use of the Word?
4. How many different Bible study methods can you identify? How many have you used?
5. What are some practical values of Bible memorization? Can you describe your practice of memorizing selected verses?

CHAPTER 10

PARTICIPATION IN THE CHURCH

When I was converted by Christ at the age of fourteen, I sought membership in the church. I never considered solitary discipleship an option. The church had earlier prepared my parents and then my sisters and me for a decision of faith. I had received good Bible teaching and training and helpful and interesting worship opportunities. I felt accepted and loved by the people in the church even before I came to a conviction of my personal sin and made a commitment to Jesus Christ. I understood that the church existed to help persons like me decide to follow Jesus. I sensed, even prior to my decision, the joy of expressing love for Jesus in ways like the singing of hymns with others who felt assured of going to heaven because of what He had done for them. A Sunday School teacher spoke to me privately about forsaking sin and receiving Jesus Christ as my Lord and Savior. I was ready to do so because of the work of the Holy Spirit, the nurture of a dedicated Christian family, the demonstrated concern and teaching of a Christian man, and the loving fellowship of a church where I observed that faith made a difference. Baptism publicly affirmed my new life in Christ.

I have actively participated in the church since that time. That is no boast. It is a statement of fact and a testimony to the grace of God. When I left home for college, the church was there to offer me rich growth opportunities. At the time of my graduation from the University of Texas, I was ordained to the gospel ministry in the church which had assisted me in discovering and pursuing this vocational calling. Seminary training was supplemented by church staff experience while completing three seminary degrees. There has been no intermission. I am still participating in the church. As a seminary professor, I am active in the church where I am a member except when I am serving as the supply or interim pastor-preacher of another church.

Parachurch ministries have been complementary in my spiritual journey. I do not discredit any Christian ministry which is strengthening disciples, but I assign priority to the church because I believe that God intended for it to be so. Participation in the church is of major importance to disciples. As an area of discipline in discipleship, active involvement in the church must not be slighted.

His Church

Jesus is very possessive about His church. Sometimes we speak proudly about "our" churches. Pastors may say, "This is what happened at *my* church." Perhaps we should have a sense of ownership; or at least a positive feeling about belonging to the congregation where we are members, but always the church really belongs to our Lord Jesus Christ. We are in it because of Him. He said, "And I tell you that you are Peter, and on this rock I will build my church, and the gates of Hades will not overcome it" (Mt. 16:18). He was not telling Peter the church was his, nor is it yours or mine. Jesus built it starting with the first disciples, and He continues to build it today.

Jesus calls sinners to Himself, to become His disciples, and then calls them into the church. The Greek word translated "church" in the New Testament is *ecclesia*, and it literally means "called out ones."[1] He calls us to live a holy life in the company of those committed to following Him (Cf.1 Tim. 1:8-9). He summons believers to unite in faith and in devotion to Him. He called the Twelve to be the church in embryonic form, to be in fellowship with Him and each other, and to start learning to carry out His mission in His power (Mt. 10:1-42). Later, He called and empowered the seventy-two with similar instructions as an indication of the future expansion of the church and its work (Lk. 10:1-20). His church in fetal form continued to develop so that at least 500 disciples, men and women, met Him on a mountain in Galilee after His resurrection and before His ascension (1 Cor. 15:6; Mt. 28:5-10, 16).[2] In commissioning them, He was ordering the whole church to make disciples in all nations (Mt. 28:19-20). About a hundred and twenty believers were gathered in Jerusalem in the days following His ascension (Acts 1:15). They prayed, chose Matthias to replace Judas, and received the filling of the Holy Spirit. The church was born! The mission began to be carried out as disciples were made from many nations starting on the day of Pentecost (Acts 2).

The predominant use of *ecclesia* in the New Testament is to identify

---

[1]Cf. K. D. Schmidt, *Ecclesia*, *TDNT*, 3:501-36. Schmidt emphasizes "assembly": "God assembles His own," 505, and the church as "a body of Christians," 504. Also see P. S. Minear, "Church, Idea of" *The Interpreter's Dictionary of the Bible*, 1:607-17.

[2]Many problems exist in harmonizing the resurrection appearances recorded in the Gospels and Acts. No attempt is made here to deal with them.

a local body of believers in a certain place such as "the church of God in Corinth" or "the church of the Thessalonians." The reference is to those who were gathered to Christ, that is, true believers, even when they are not assembled. Sometimes the plural "churches" is used and indicates believers in a section of the country like the region of Macedonia or Galatia (2 Cor. 8:1; Gal. 1:2). While a few references to the church universal may be observed, the emphasis is on local churches in which Christ may be seen to be at work through the Spirit. This is the cutting edge of Christianity where believers relate to the Lord, to each other, and to the community in which they are living as Christians.

Three Images of His Church

The church is the **body of Christ** (Col. 1:18, 24; 1 Cor. 12:27; Eph. 1:22-23, 5:23). He is its head. What image could have been selected to better depict the relationship between Christ and His church? It is uniquely and especially His. Our English word "church" comes from the Greek *kuriakon* which means "that which belongs to the Lord."[3] A close affinity exists between every member of the body and Jesus Christ the head. Our invisible Lord achieves some visibility in this world through His people when they are assembled or functioning together toward a common purpose. Paul explained, "Just as each of us has one body with many members, and these members do not all have the same function, so in Christ we who are many form one body, and each member belongs to all the others" (Rom. 12:4). Every disciple has a dependent and subordinate relation to Jesus and an interdependent relation to other Christians. The church does not save, but the saved comprise the church, the body of Christ. Discipleship is not a private enterprise. We must do it together, and active participation by all is expected. Submission and obedience to Christ by every member are needed for effective functioning.

Also, the church is the **building of Christ**. We often speak of "the church building," meaning the material structure of wood or brick or stone. That use of "church" is never found in the Scriptures. The church existed for two hundred years without church buildings. In a more dynamic way, the church made up of all the followers of Christ is His building (1 Cor. 3:9). Paul asked, "Don't you know that you yourselves

---

[3]Minear, *TIDB*, 1:607.

are God's temple and that God's Spirit lives in you?" (1 Cor. 3:16). The only foundation for the church is Christ, and the chief occupant of the church is the Holy Spirit. Likewise, Peter addressed God's elect in various places saying, "You also, like living stones, are being built into a spiritual house" (1 Pet. 2:5). We are to allow Him to put us together and build us up. Our part is to be *living* stones, centering our lives in Him who is the Life.

A third image of the church which stresses our belonging to the Lord is that of **His purchase.** Jesus bought us by His death for our salvation from sin. Paul declared this when he challenged the Ephesian elders with these words: "Be shepherds of the church of God which he bought with his own blood" (Acts 20:28). In prospect, the church would belong to Him, so He gave Himself over to death to purify it from sin. The call to participation in the church is based on the memory of the dear price the Savior paid to secure the church for Himself.

These three images, the body, the building and the purchase, all highlight the church as belonging to Christ.[4] Each believer belongs to Him and is accepted into His church, which is the assembly of all of His called out ones. Both individually and corporately, we are His for Him to control and direct as He sees fit. We are charged to participate in His mission as surely as the first disciples were called to share in it. That is what being His church means.

Our Fellowship

The New Testament also describes the church as a fellowship. We belong to Christ and we belong with each other. The Greek word *koinonia* may be translated fellowship or partnership. It carries the idea of joint participation. My wife and I are described legally as "joint tenants with rights in common." We insist on that arrangement. Everything I own, she owns. There is no distinction as far as property rights or financial holdings. In the church we Christians are equals and share jointly all the privileges and responsibilities of our union with Christ and with each other.

The first use of *koinonia* in the New Testament is in the description of life in the Jerusalem church when it was first born. The baptized believers "devoted themselves to the apostles' teaching and to the

---

4Other images for the church in the NT are discussed by Minear, *TIDB*, 1:609-16.

fellowship, to the breaking of bread and to prayer" (Acts 2:42). What follows is an enlargement of the picture of fellowship: worship, miraculous events, sharing possessions to meet each other's needs, meeting in each other's homes with joy and praise, winning confidence from others, and assimilating new converts (Acts 2:43-47). Exciting! You know it was. We do not know how long it lasted, but we wish something similar were happening in every city and church in the world today.

Paul used the word "fellowship" in writing to the Corinthian church. He promised them, "God, who has called you into fellowship with His Son Jesus Christ our Lord, is faithful" (1 Cor. 1:9). The problem that grieved Paul most, and that he addressed first, was divisions in the fellowship. The members were dividing what God had united. Warring factions had supplanted the loving unity. Any church is in serious trouble when fellowship is destroyed. In contrast, the Philippian church brought Paul great pleasure. He wrote to them, "In all my prayers for all of you, I always pray with joy because of your partnership [*koinonia*] in the gospel from the first day until now" (Phil. 1:4-5). Nevertheless, Paul appealed to two women in the church to settle their differences so that their fellowship might be restored (Phil. 4:2).

Every Christian should participate in the church in such a loving and harmonious way that the fellowship of all the believers is strengthened. That does not rule out the possibility of disagreements, but it does ask for elimination of an ugly, contentious spirit. Mutual respect and tender regard are needed always, particularly when opposing views are being stated. Such a response in times of controversy is not natural. That is why this response provides such an impressive witness to the grace of God in His people when it does occur.

Our fellowship in the church is designed to be a family fellowship. In times of such epidemic abuse, conflict, and divorce in families, one unacquainted with the Scriptures might not understand. Ties in the Jewish family were typically strong and close. Christians, even in a pagan culture, were directed to establish an exclusive and enduring bond between marriage partners and a nurturing relationship of parents toward their children. The church was to be a model in its relationships for harmony in the homes. In one of Paul's exhortations to a church, he wrote,

Therefore, as God's chosen people, holy and dearly loved, clothe yourselves with compassion, kindness, humility, gentleness and patience. Bear with each other and forgive whatever grievances you may have against one another. Forgive as the Lord forgave you. And over all these virtues put on love, which binds them together in perfect unity (Col. 3:12-14).

Another family word Paul uses is *oikeios* translated "family" or "household" from *oikos* (house). In Gal. 6:10 he pleads, "Let us do good to all people, especially to those who belong to the family of believers." It is not just blood lines that cause us to experience "family." Likewise, we do not automatically realize family togetherness when we are saved. In both biological and spiritual families, positive participation together is what enables us to enjoy fellowship. When Christians act in coopera-tion with each other and have the spirit of Christ, a higher dimension of unity is possible. Jesus said, "Whoever does the will of my Father in heaven is my brother and sister and mother" (Mt. 12:50). Thus joined to Jesus, we are in closer proximity to one another and may know "family" in its truest sense.

"Brothers" is another family term used in the New Testament to speak of the church. In Acts alone it is used thirty times in addressing the assembled believers. Jesus had said to His disciples, "You have only one Master and you are all brothers" (Mt. 23:8). To be His brother is to be a fellow heir with Him and all the faithful of an everlasting inheritance (Rom. 8:17; Eph. 1:18). Sibling rivalry and competition do not enter the biblical picture of brothers at all.

Another biblical concept which expresses our fellowship is that of "fellow workers" (*sunergoi*). Paul was expressing the equal status and joint participation in the ministry at Corinth of Apollos and perhaps others when he said, "We are God's fellow workers" (1 Cor. 3:9). Later he included Timothy with himself when he spoke of them as "God's fellow workers" (2 Cor. 6:1; 1 Th. 3:2). They shared in a ministry. As each church member exercises his or her role in the work of the Lord, a camaraderie grows between them. Working together in His church breaks down barriers and strengthens relationships. Generally, the more people there are who are actively involved in the work of the church, the better the fellowship will be.

All Are Laity

Church renewal in our time has been inspired by a rediscovery of the laity. Every branch of Christendom has been affected. All of the people (*laos*) of God are laity. Some have special callings and gifts for leadership. Leaders are among the people, working with and for the rest of the people. No hierarchy of church authority is described. This concept has been liberating for many church pastors and leaders as well as other church members. The leaders are freed from carrying so much of the responsibility for the church alone and the members are permitted to participate more fully in the mission of the church.

In the Old Testament, Israel was called the people of God. The sermon of Moses to all Israel included these words, "The Lord your God has chosen you out of all the peoples on the face of the earth to be his people, his treasured possession" (Dt. 7:6). Because of His love, God made a covenant with the nation, blessed it when it was obedient to Him and punished its disobedience.

In the New Testament this same God reveals an expanded provision to make disciples in all nations. All who repent and believe in Jesus are saved and become children of God. His church is His people. The covenant is renewed. Christ's blood atones potentially for the sins of the whole world. The church is made up of those cleansed by His blood. Gentile members are not inferior to Jewish members. Christ "has made the two one" (Eph. 2:14). As Paul indicated, "His purpose was to create in himself one new man out of the two" (Eph. 2:15). This infers Jesus' plan to form a new kind of Christian community. He gave equal standing to all in His church; the highest office is that of servant or disciple. Peter gave the laity prominence in penning these words to fellow believers,

> You are a chosen people, a royal priesthood, a holy nation, a people belonging to God, that you may declare the praises of him who called you out of darkness into his wonderful light. Once you were not a people, but now you are the people of God; once you had not received mercy, but now you have received mercy (1 Pet. 2:9-10).

This biblical text has been used to teach the priesthood of all believers also, which is a related idea. The focus, however, is obviously on "the people of God." You are a man of God or you are a woman of God or you are a youth or child of God and we all are laity, the people of God.

With this privilege comes responsibility. As the verses quoted above said, praise and worship are primary. A part of this worship is to be the repeated commemoration of the death of Jesus in the Lord's Supper (Mk.

14:22-25; 1 Cor. 11:23-26). Another duty is to assemble regularly with God's people to encourage them toward love and good deeds (Heb. 10:24-25). Regular giving, likewise, is assigned so that needs may be met and grace may be demonstrated (2 Cor. 8:1-7; 9:6-15). The message of God's grace shown us in Christ can hardly be communicated by a selfish congregation. The obligation to pray for others also belongs to church members (Eph. 6:18). Participation in decisions pertaining to the fulfilling of the church's mission is to be shared by the whole church (Acts 6:1-6; 15:22-35). That means that every member is to become informed and to act wisely regarding church business. Furthermore, the entire church is accountable for evangelism and missions, spreading the truth about Jesus in order to make disciples around the neighborhood and around the world (Mt. 28:19-20; Acts 1:8). All the people of God are called to be the church, the called-out ones, on mission assignment from Jesus Christ. Every Christian is a missionary. The responsibilities of church membership need to be taught carefully to all the members and retaught at different stages in life.

Spiritual Gifts

God has provided gifts to all the members of the church so that they can participate helpfully. The ideal is for each one to serve in the church according to his or her gift(s). The variety of spiritual gifts mentioned in the New Testament indicates numerous ministries that may be performed by gifted members. A common error is to think of spiritual gifts as only applying to professional leaders in the church such as pastors and staff. Faithful teaching of the Word will enable members to see that they too are gifted by God and have important functions to perform.

A spiritual gift is a talent or ability given by God to be used in a spiritual ministry to build up the church. Every Christian has at least one spiritual gift (1 Cor. 12:7). Numerous gifts may be seen being utilized by the same person. The apostle Paul, for example, possessed many. The number of gifts a person or church has is not an indication of maturity or superiority. The immature Corinthian church had many spiritual gifts. (1 Cor. 1:7). Gifts are not rewards but are evidence of the grace of God. The Greek word translated spiritual gifts (*charismata*) has "grace" (*charis*) in it, so they are literally "grace-gifts." When a spiritual ministry is being performed, the Holy Spirit is manifesting His presence. The purpose of God in giving spiritual gifts is the building up of the church, the body of Christ. A valid test, therefore, of the proper use of any spiritual gift is whether or not the church is blessed by its use.

No definitive list of spiritual gifts is supplied, but four New Testament passages mention specific gifts. They are Rom. 12:6-8, 1 Cor. 12-14, Eph. 4:11-13 and 1 Pet. 4:10-11. At least nineteen different gifts are named. There are several types such as speaking, leading, serving, evangelizing and possibly others. I do not consider these lists to exclude other gifts from being added. Whatever needs the church has in any time and place, God by His Spirit will raise up believers with gifts to meet those needs. Music, writing, and child care are areas of giftedness, for instance, that we see being used to build up the church at present, though they are not specifically mentioned in the Scriptures. If any of the gifts, such as tongues, are extinct now, this, in my opinion, cannot be determined by accurate Scriptural interpretation. I am convinced, however, that tongues-speaking is not essential to salvation or to worship, and not a proof of being Spirit-filled or baptized in the Spirit. There is not one spiritual gift that is essential to salvation, but love and prophecy are mentioned as desirable for all (1 Cor. 12:31-13:3; 14:1).

All Christians should view themselves as functioning members of the body of Christ, not more or less important to the body than any other (1 Cor. 12:12-27). Discovering one's spiritual gift(s) becomes then a major responsibility. How does one proceed to do this? An individual studies the Scriptural teaching about spiritual gifts, investigates the needs of the church, prays for God's guidance, attempts to perform some service or ministry in the church, and evaluates the results. This is not different from the procedure the pastor has gone through, likely, in ascertaining God's call to his ministry. A member may function in different capacities according to the church's needs and his or her abilities.

The disciplined development of a gift may be necessary even though it is divinely bestowed. A preacher may still learn to preach better and may be trained to do so. A teacher may sharpen skills by study and practice. An administrator may acquire knowledge of organization and leadership that will improve performance. A seminary does not distribute spiritual gifts, obviously, but it may assist gifted students in achieving a greater effectiveness in the employment of their gifts. Likewise, the church should offer teaching and training to its members that will enable them to use their gifts to better advantage.

Members are accountable to use their spiritual gift(s) for the building up of the church. Peter wrote, "Each one should use whatever gift he has received to serve others, faithfully administering God's grace in its various forms" (1 Pet. 4:10). The praise and honor of Jesus Christ are the ultimate goal of the building of His body. "To him be the glory and the power for ever and ever. Amen" (1 Pet. 4:11).

Two warnings with regard to the use of spiritual gifts need to be added. First, avoid exalting any gift above the Giver. The Holy Spirit is Himself the supreme gift and the Giver of gifts (Acts 2:38). Second, avoid excusing disobedience because of perceived absence of special gifts. Obey the commands of your Lord, such as to exercise faith, give generously, serve cheerfully, and witness regularly, regardless of whether or not you feel you have received a spiritual gift for doing those things. A lack of special giftedness does not exempt a believer from obedience to the clear commands set out in the Scriptures.

Growing the Church

Concentrating on our own spiritual growth and assisting others in their Christian development is one of the finest ways open to us to grow our churches. Other types of church growth such as expansion and extension are also worthy of attention, but not to be ignored is a plan for strengthening the character and convictions, the personality and proficiency of each member of the congregation.

Leaders with varied spiritual gifts are provided to the church by Jesus so that all may "grow up into him who is the Head, that is Christ" (Eph. 4:15).[5] Christlikeness is the goal. That defines maturity, the finished product of the church enterprise. God's people are being prepared for works of service. Their faith in and knowledge of the Son of God should be evolving so that "windy" teachers and preachers do not lead them to accept false doctrine. Instead, they should show an increasing ability to converse intelligently about Christian concerns while revealing a good grasp of the Scriptures, "speaking the truth in love" (Eph. 4:15). Their ability to cooperate in the accomplishment of the Christian mission should be apparent. Significant interrelatedness in the body of Christ is

---

[5]No passage of Scripture has been more influential in lay and church renewal than Eph. 4:11-16.

vital to the church's outreach in the world.[6]

Let us grow our churches by growing ourselves. Fruitful discipleship will result in fruitful churches. People who are progressing spiritually do not create problems; they solve them. They are not spectators but participants. They are not critics but are becoming Christlike. They are not takers but givers, not power-pursuers but servants. They are doers of the Word and not hearers only. God bless them and multiply them!

A vision of the church as it is meant to be is valuable to every congregation and its leaders. How will we know when the church is mature? We do not see any examples of perfect churches in the New Testament. The churches at Thessalonica (1 Th. 1:2-10), at Smyrna (Rev. 2:8-11), at Philadelphia (Rev. 3:7-13), and at Philippi (Phil. 1:3-11), however, are worthy of emulation in significant aspects. Sufficient information is available through serious Bible study to enable us to know what kind of maturity God desires for His people in every assembly. Form your own vision in this manner and patiently pray and work to make it a reality in your church. Remember,

Christ loved the church and gave himself up for her to make her holy, cleansing her by the washing with water through the word and to present her to himself as a radiant church, without stain or wrinkle or any other blemish, but holy and blameless (Eph. 5:25-27).

That is church maturity. Only Christ can produce it, but He is already at work in every church to that glorious end. He wants to use us in the project.

Study Questions

1. In what sense does the church belong to Jesus Christ?
2. Which is your favorite image of the church found in the New Testament? Why?
3. What kind of activity is suggested by the use of the word "fellowship" to describe the church? How does that relate to concepts of family?

---

[6]Neill Q. Hamilton, *Maturing in the Christian Life: A Pastor's Guide* (Philadelphia: The Geneva Press, 1984). Hamilton has a good emphasis on the pastor's role of helping members toward maturity. I disagree, however, with his use on pages 43-45 of "discipleship" as a self-centered phase of the Christian life rather than the whole.

4. What are the implications of stating that all of God's people are laity?
5. How does the use of spiritual gifts enable the church to carry out its assignment?
6. Can you discuss church growth in terms of spiritual development?

His Calling
(Matthew 4:18-25)

I wonder if I would have left my net
And all that I planned to be,
If Jesus had come where I plied my trade
And had said, "Come, follow me."

I wonder if I would have left my dad
Like those guys, James and John,
For no doubt he thought they must be insane.
Jesus called, and they were gone.

I will never know what I would have done
Had I been there in their place,
But by faith I've seen what I think they saw—
The love in the Master's face.

— Ed Thiele

PART THREE

GOD'S EXPECTATIONS AND OUR CHALLENGE

God who created us and saved us through the death and resurrection of His Son has high expectations for us. He knows our potential because of what He has done for us and what He stands ready to do with us and in us. We may share this optimistic outlook about our growth as disciples because of our faith in Him. As the Apostle Paul wrote, "Being confident of this, that he who began a good work in you will carry it on to completion until the day of Christ Jesus" (Phil. 1:6).

In the four chapters that remain we will think about love, servanthood, disciplemaking, and victory in spiritual warfare. Our greatest challenge may be to excel in these areas. The maturity of Christians is truly tested by our response to God's instructions in these matters.

CHAPTER 11

LOVE AMONG DISCIPLES

Jesus told His first disciples that one activity would identify them to others as His disciples—love. He had gotten up from the table where He was sharing the Passover meal with them and with a towel around His waist and a wash basin in His hands, He washed their feet. He told them they should be willing to do that for each other. Then He said,

My children, I will be with you only a little longer . . . A new command I give you: Love one another. As I have loved you, so you must love one another. By this all men will know that you are my disciples, if you love one another (Jn. 13:33-35).

Is there any way Jesus could have made the emphasis stronger? He first showed them "the full extent of his love" (Jn. 13:1) and then commanded them to love each other as He had loved them. He declared that love would be the distinguishing characteristic by which everyone would know whose disciples they were.

Bumper stickers, rear window decals, badges, T-shirts, and pendants are currently being used to mark some as believers in Jesus, but no insignia can communicate one's belonging to Christ as effectively as love being lived out in daily experience. Styles and fashions change, but there is an enduring quality about Christian love that transcends these passing fads. What Jesus said to His first disciples is just as true and important to us today. We will never convince anyone that we are disciples of Jesus if we are lacking in love.

Love for God

The capacity for love in human beings originated with God. He created us to care. When He made us in His own likeness, He shared responsibility with us, an act of love. The first man and woman were given duties to perform by which they might show grateful acknowledgement and affection for Him their Creator. They were given responsibility for each other to live in unity. Their disobedience of His command was a rejection of His loving authority over their lives. When temptation came, they did not protect each other but jointly violated the covenant of love God had made with them. For this He punished them but still loved them. Already He had a plan to restore sinners to a loving relationship with Himself.

The first commandment in importance, Jesus said, is "Love the Lord your God with all your heart and with all your soul and with all your mind and with all your strength" (Mk. 12:30).[1] Obviously, only a total, unconditional love for God fulfills that commandment. Love for God every day in every situation is imperative. If we have not committed any other sins, we are all law-breakers at that point. Indeed, every sin is an evidence of failure to love God enough. Even the secret sins of thought and feeling reveal a deficiency in love for God.

Trust, worship, and obedience are the ways God has given us of proving our love for Him. "Without faith it is impossible to please God" (Heb. 11:6). Loving Him with our hearts and minds surely includes believing that He is the only God and rejecting any possible rivals for that affection and allegiance which belong to Him. Worship and adoration flow with genuine love for Him. Bowing down to Him with reverence, cherishing each thought of Him, being eager to serve Him—these are signs of true devotion. Obedience also reveals that we hold Him in the highest esteem and have no desire to live contrary to His will. In one of Moses' speeches he exhorted Israel, "Love the Lord your God and keep his requirements, his decrees, his laws and his commands always" (Dt. 11:1). Jesus called for the same response when He said, "If you love me, you will obey what I command" (Jn. 14:15). We have no more pressing obligation or glorious privilege than to live with love for God.

Love among Christians

Loving God makes possible our loving other people in a unique way. The atheist or non-Christian may profess and practice love for other people, but there will always be a void in any human relationship that does not have love for God as its foundation. One's relationship to God powerfully affects every other personal relationship. Christians united in love for God have a solid basis on which to build the most meaningful and satisfying love relationship.

The word for love used most in the New Testament, *agape,* generally

---

[1]Note that Mt. 22:37 omits "strength" but Lk. 10:25 and Dt. 6:5 include it.

indicates a self-giving love. This is the kind of love with which God has loved us in giving His Son through the cross for our salvation.[2] *Agape* is used of God's love, Jesus' love, and disciples' love. Another word *phileo* (verb), is used more often where love for a friend or family member is indicated. Nowhere in the Scriptures are these words defined, so the interpretation is determined by the use. We are loved with the unselfish love of God the Father and God the Son, and we are command-ed to love each other with that same kind of love.[3] Jesus prayed that the love which the Father has for Him may be found in His disciples (Jn. 17:26).

A Closer Examination of Agape

Because love is so important to disciples, I am always searching for a better definition of it. Someone long ago taught me to think of it as "an inward openness to the needs of others." I like that, but it is incomplete. *Agape* is more than an inner attitude. Erich Fromm described it as self-giving. He wrote, "The most precious gift any person can give another is the gift of self—the gift of one's joy, one's knowledge, one's feelings, one's hurts, one's interests, even one's honor."[4] Yes, love is attitudes and actions that portray the giving of self for the good of another. Is that not the way God loves us? "Unconquerable benevolence, invincible good will" is William Barclay's definition of *agape*, particularly as seen in God's love for us.[5] Still another writer who helps us understand this wonderful quality that should mark the life of every Christian is Morton Kelsey. He wrote,

> The love that we are talking about refers to that complex of emotions, attitudes, movements of will and actions in which we reach out to others in a caring, concerned manner, desiring to let other people know that we care about them and wish to facilitate the achievement of their potential.[6]

---

[2] See Jn. 3:16; 15:13; Rom. 5:8; Eph. 2:4.

[3] See Rom. 12:9; Eph. 5:2; 1 Th. 3:12.

[4] Erich Fromm, *The Art of Loving* (New York: Harper and Row, 1956), 20.

[5] William Barclay, *More New Testament Words* (London: SCM, 1948), 16.

[6] Morton T. Kelsey, *Caring: How Can We Love One Another?* (New York: Paulist, 1981), 15.

The only way to really know the meaning of *agape* is in experience. As we realize God's love for us and as we give ourselves to and for God and other people, we shall progressively learn what love is. By this process we shall also understand why it is the greatest thing in the world and the fruit of the Spirit.[7]

A Look at 1 John 4:7-5:5

My beginning Greek course in the seminary was a study in the biblical language of the first letter of John, the beloved Apostle. This book was chosen because of the simplicity of its vocabulary. Words like sin and light and love are repeated many times. Simple though it is in language, however, the letter is profound in meaning. The appeal for love among Christians which it contains in 1 Jn. 4:7-5:5 is very compelling. Let us examine it more closely.

1. **The source of love is God.** John knew that those in fellowship with God the Father and Jesus His Son had the capacity to love unselfishly. Through their relationship to God, the believers could become expressions of self-giving love. "Love comes from God," he wrote (4:7). We may feel that it is not possible for us to love a certain person or group. Perhaps this is so, but it is possible for God, and by His Spirit we can love them also.
2. **The divine nature is loving.** "God is love" (4:8, 16) is repeated in this passage. Love is the essence of His being. Nothing He ever did was inconsistent with love, and we can be certain He will never act contrary to love. We are able to love God and to be loved by God because He is love.
3. **The fullest expression of God's love is in Christ.** We have solid historical evidence presented in Jesus' life, death, and resurrection that God's love for all people is real. God did not wait for us to love Him or to be worthy of His love. He loved us first.

This is how God showed his love among us: He sent his one and only Son into the world that we might live through him. This is love: not that we loved God, but that he loved us and sent his Son

---

[7]See Henry Drummond, *The Greatest Thing in the World* (Mount Vernon, NY: Peter Pauper, n.d.) and Gal. 5:22.

as an atoning sacrifice for our sins (1 Jn. 4:9-10).

The Gospels are history and yet more than history to us. We accept by faith the record that Jesus was God in this world as a man showing love in order to rescue believing sinners for eternal life.[8]

4. **If we love one another as we should, we have grounds for confidence that God lives in us and that we live in Him** (4:11-13). Without loving each other in a supernatural way, what sign is there that we share the life of the God of love? However, if we are truly loving, others can see that we have been spiritually born as children of God and that we know Him experientially (4:7-8).

5. **No fear of condemnation at a future divine judgment should be present in the believer who is mature in love.** God desires to make us like Himself so that we can face judgment confidently, assured of salvation by His grace. As love grows, fear can diminish (4:17-18).

6. **Hatred of a brother and love for God cannot commingle.** "If anyone says, 'I love God,' yet hates his brother, he is a liar" (1 Jn. 4:20). Lovers of God must love their brothers also. In the family of God, we are not free to select as brothers those whom we feel deserve our love and despise the rest. If we love the Father, we will love His children as well (1 Jn. 5:1-2). Differences of race, language, nationality or denomination should not separate members of the Father's family.

7. **Obedience to God's commands demonstrates love for God.** We best show our love for God by obeying Him as our Father. This is not a painful assignment. As believers in Jesus, we have victory over the sinful world and are free to live in love.

Action is Essential

Love is something one does. Disciples too often have been misled to think that Christian love is being demonstrated when a "warm, fuzzy" feeling is maintained. As pointed out earlier, emotions and attitudes may be involved, but primarily love must be exhibited in actions. "Love your neighbor" cannot be obeyed without effort. Remember that Jesus illustrated how to do this by describing the behavior of the Good Samaritan (Lk. 10:30-35). Better still, He depicted love in all He did,

---

[8]See also 1 Jn. 4:14.

especially by giving Himself over to sacrificial death. The call to discipleship is to do as He did, to act sacrificially. Jesus told the Twelve, "Greater love has no one than this, that he lay down his life for his friends" (Jn. 15:13).

The application demands action. Love is the root of all Christian ethics. Baking cakes and pies for someone, going to console another who is grieving, teaching literacy to someone who cannot read and write English, and confronting one who is abusing oneself or another person are just a few ways to practice love. John presented another example, as follows:

> If anyone has material possessions and sees his brother in need but has no pity on him, how can the love of God be in him? Dear children, let us not love with words or tongue but with actions and truth (1 Jn. 3:17-18).

Kelsey stated, "Morality, ethics, and Christian action are simply allowing that love to move out through us to other human beings in various circumstances."[9] To open ourselves up to the love of God and to become channels of that love to others is the nature of Christian ministry. Loving is not a job for the lazy, although God is loving through us.

A Brief Study of 1 Corinthians 13

One of the most familiar chapters in the Bible must be this one. Ray Summers gave me this three-point outline for it: The Preeminence of Love, 1-3; The Practice of Love, 4-8a; and The Permanence of Love, 8b-13. As we are thinking about love in action just now, I want you to review with me the middle verses, 4-8a. Love is known by what it does and does not do.

Notice the positive features first. Love acts with patience. Self-restraint and endurance are elements in patience. It keeps on doing the right thing, even if favorable results are not immediately obtained.

"Love is kind" (13:4). Thoughtful and helpful words and deeds demonstrate the presence of love. Sympathetic and benevolent responses to human needs manifest it.

Love is happy when truth is being spoken and done (13:6). "Speaking

---

[9]Kelsey, 37.

the truth in love" (Eph. 4:15) and living "a life of love" (Eph. 5:2) are ways to imitate God "as dearly loved children" (Eph. 5:1). John wrote, "It has given me great joy to find some of your children walking in the truth" (2 Jn. 4).

Also, love "always protects, always trusts, always hopes, always perseveres" (13:7). What an array of positive practices that includes! Love takes responsibility for the security of others, places confidence in others, expects the best from others, and demonstrates tenacity even in adverse circumstances.

The positive features of love are impressive but so are those expressed negatively. Love is not proud, rude, self-seeking, or easily angered (13:4-5), and it does not envy, boast, keep records on wrongdoing, delight in evil, nor fail (13:4-8a). This is what the Apostle labels "the most excellent way" (1 Cor. 12:31). Who but Jesus ever lived up to such an exalted ideal? Nevertheless, we must be fellow-climbers trekking toward that peak and assisting one another. "Let us consider how we may spur one another on toward love and good deeds" (Heb. 10:24).

The Case for Self-love

Jesus never did command us to love ourselves, but He seemed to take it for granted that we would. He said, "Love your neighbor as yourself" (Mt. 22:39). The right kind of self-love is wholesome. A person normally takes care of oneself, defends oneself, feeds and clothes oneself, and in other ways shows that one regards one's life and well-being as a positive value. We sin by not placing a high enough value on others. One needs self-esteem in order to be able to practice self-giving love (*agape*).

The knowledge of God's love for us and of Christ's death for us should make us feel valued. In spite of the past transgressions we have committed which so deflate our sense of personal value, Christ brought us forgiveness and cleansing. All of God's provisions for us and promises to us are designed to make us feel worthy. The calling by Jesus to be involved with Him in the discipling of the nations surely indicates that our Lord respects us and our potential for usefulness. Moreover, the gifts to us of the Holy Spirit and eternal life encourage us to think positively about ourselves. We are children of the King of kings and Lord of lords.

We are never told to take a dim view of ourselves. Paul declared,

Do nothing out of selfish ambition or vain conceit, but in humility consider others better than yourselves. Each of you should look not only to your own interests, but also to the interests of others (Phil. 2:3-4).

Humility does not come with thinking bad things about ourselves or minimizing what we through grace might be able to accomplish. Humility rather concentrates on helping others to be all that they can be and seeks to remain submissive to God. We need a realistic understanding of our strengths and weaknesses and a genuine interest in other people. A healthy self-love makes it possible for us to love our neighbors. A valid goal is to be a happy, healthy Christian person for the sake of loving and serving God and others.

Confronting Hindrances

True *agape* does not flow freely in most connections between persons. Lives intersect frequently in business, social, and even religious encounters without love being a factor. Many hindrances must exist since this is so. I am only going to discuss two major ones, pride and fear.

Pride is centering one's life in oneself. Contrary to healthy self-love, pride is arrogance, a feeling of superiority to others, an inflated sense of one's own importance. Pride devalues other people. This was a particular problem for the Pharisees of Jesus' time on earth. Recall the story Jesus told of the contrast between the Pharisee and the tax collector who went up to the temple to pray. The Pharisee's prayer was essentially self-congratulatory and he viewed the tax collector with contempt.[10] With self-righteous haughtiness, Pharisees looked down on everyone else. Whether one's pride is based on lineage, the size and location of one's house, job and salary, social status, children and grandchildren, or whatever, if anything elevates the individual's worth as a human being above that of others in one's own eyes, pride has caused an alienation and prevented love from being present.

Pride of race and nationality are barriers to an interchange of love. Hitler's name will always be a reminder to us of how far off track and how destructive such pride can become. Even tribes and families of the same race and nationality can be separated into rival camps spewing

---

[10]Lk. 18:9-14.

hatred on one another. A part of the power of the gospel is its ability to break down walls of division created by pride and to unite differing peoples in love. Jews and Gentiles, slaves and their masters, Greeks and Ethiopians could experience brotherly love in Christ.

The other major hindrance to love is **fear**. Individuals tend to be afraid of being themselves and opening up to others in relationships. To really love others is to become vulnerable. One can be rejected, ridiculed, even persecuted as a result of revealing one's thoughts, feelings, hopes, values, and beliefs. It is safer to remain anonymous. Risking is an essential part of letting love control our relationships. What pleasant surprises are in store for the Christian who, under the leadership of the Spirit, reaches out to others with authentic interest. Tactful questioning and careful listening are keys to effective communication. Strangers may quickly become friends. The alternatives are indifference and superficiality, neither of which is a Christian quality.

The fear of bodily harm could be what deters us from caring enough about another person to converse or attempt to help. More often, however, the fear is that we will lose time or convenience by giving ourselves to another. That is a valid consideration. Such fear is probably what motivated the priest and the Levite to pass by on the other side of the road and to fail to love their neighbor. I can identify with that. They might have been late for the "service." But look at what riches are missed by failing to respond to another's need—the chance to serve, the experience of love given and received, the joy of the Lord. Robert Browning wrote,

> For life, with all it yields of joy and woe,
> And hope and fear,—believe the aged friend—
> Is just a chance o' the prize of learning love.[11]

We do not have to let pride and fear rob us of the blessing of being conduits for Christ's love.

---

[11]Browning, 90.

Love in the Family

Disciples will seldom have a greater opportunity to give and receive love than in their families. To make one's home a warm haven of Christian love is one of the aims of discipleship. Generally speaking, no home should be happier than that of a Christian family, and in both sadness and happiness, love should prevail. This requires making time available to be with each other, not just living in the same house, but paying attention to each other. Love means trying to understand each other and to relate constructively. It means very little to say we love everyone in the world. It is much more difficult and at the same time rewarding to try to love one person at a time. In the family is a good place to start. As Kelsey wrote, "Everyone of us needs a place where we are accepted and considered valuable whether we are right or wrong."[12]

Marriage was created by God for intimate sharing. Jesus was reminding us of that when He said of the married couple, "They are no longer two, but one" (Mt. 19:6). Self-giving love is absolutely essential to marriage maintenance. We can become so preoccupied with our roles and with other duties and interests, that we neglect each other. The command is clear: "Husbands, love (*agapate*) your wives, just as Christ loved the church and gave himself up for her" (Eph. 5:25), and the same paragraph ends, "the wife must respect her husband" (Eph. 5:33). A married disciple cannot afford to give anything except love for God priority above this obligation. The quality of love expressed in the husband-wife relationship determines the spiritual and emotional climate in the home.

More single and previously married parents are raising children alone than ever before in our country. The challenge to offer adequate love to each child is all the greater when parenting alone, and the grace of God is obviously needed. The love relationship between the solo parent and God becomes all the more crucial.

The love of parents for their children should be self-giving but not overly permissive. Limits have to be set for the welfare of the child, and discipline will often be necessary to reinforce the limits. Discipline does not require physical punishment, which should be used sparingly, if at all. Children learn the right way much better by positive guidance and encouragement and reward. We are tempted to punish in anger and

---

[12]Kelsey, 105.

frustration instead of in love. Love looks for creative ways to punish and tries to correct by suggesting alternative actions. A loving parent should refuse to react with harsh criticism and sarcasm. The cardinal rule in parenting is to be sure the child feels loved by you. Whatever religious training is given in the home and the church will be interpreted by the child in terms of the example of the parents, especially in regard to love.

Promoting Love in Your Church

Every disciple of Jesus wants to belong to a loving church. As I wrote earlier, God desires this for every believer. Whether you would describe your present church as loving or not, there are probably some things you could do to promote love in the congregation. This ought to be a major objective of every pastor and church leader. Let me suggest seven things which I believe would be helpful.

1. **Be a loving person**. This comes easier for some than others, but it is the obligation of all. Reach out to others. Find out about them. Get to know them. Show them that you value them. Try to meet some of their needs.
2. **Pray for others**. Be specific. Invite others to share their requests with you so that you can intercede for them. Encourage them to pray for each other.
3. **Preach and teach about love**. Lead Bible studies on the subject. Use the theme of love for a conference or retreat. Sponsor courses on marriage enrichment and parenting skills. Call attention to books and tapes on this subject that you have found helpful and lend them to others.
4. **Plan for the affectionate assimilation of new members**. Be sure that they are genuinely welcomed and made to feel their importance in the family of the faithful. Assist them in forming new friendships.
5. **Deal maturely with fellowship problems**. When you learn of hurt feelings and broken relationships in the membership, offer to listen patiently and non-judgmentally. Trust the power of God's love to bring peace and healing through you.
6. **Plan social occasions** such as picnics, banquets, and receptions to foster good relationships between members and between their families. Use worship experiences, especially the Lord's Supper, to stress unity among believers.

7. **Involve members with each other** on committee assignments and in
   ministry projects according to their gifts and interests, and anticipate
   love developing among the participants. When church work is done
   together in the name of Christ, a bonding takes place among the
   workers that is very special.

You may think of other ways, but I have discovered these practices to be
very beneficial. I recommend them to you. As Paul wrote, "Love must
be sincere . . . Be devoted to one another in brotherly love" (Rom. 12:9-
10). We must never give up on helping our churches embody the love
of Jesus Christ.

The Supreme Test

Some people we know are easy to love. They are kind and considerate
and patient. We see them as being our kind of folks. Then, there are
others, people who oppose us or irritate us. They are not like us in many
ways. Showing respect for them, much less love, would seem almost like
a betrayal of ourselves and all we stand for.

Jesus told us to love our enemies. That's the supreme test. Not only
must we eliminate hatred for anyone, we must take the initiative in
loving those who are against us. Go the second mile; do more than is
required; pray for your persecutors. Do all of this so "that you may be
sons of your Father in heaven" (Mt. 5:45), because He is always sending
blessings like sunshine and rain on bad people as well as good. Then
Jesus added,

> If you love those who love you, what reward will you get? Are not
> even the tax collectors doing that? And if you greet only your
> brothers, what are you doing more than others? Do not even pagans
> do that? Be perfect, therefore, as your heavenly Father is perfect (Mt.
> 5:46-48).

Nothing short of showing God's perfect love to others, even our
antagonists, is the target toward which we are to aim our lives. We want
others to be able to discern by our actions whose children we are because
of our resemblance to the Father.

Jesus showed us how to forgive enemies. While He was on the cross
between criminals, He prayed for those who executed Him, "Father,

forgive them, for they do not know what they are doing" (Lk. 23:34). We are admonished, "Be kind and compassionate to one another, forgiving each other, just as in Christ, God forgave you" (Eph. 4:32). What a challenge it is to forgive personal injury and respond with love!

If you, in the right spirit, confront someone who has mistreated you, the conflict may be resolved, an apology made, and forgiveness extended. If, however, this approach is not successful, Jesus encouraged involving one or two witnesses and, as a last resort, even the whole church in settling the dispute and in demonstrating forgiveness (Mt. 18:15-17). Only a hardened sinner who stubbornly refuses to repent for obvious guilt should be excluded from the fellowship like an unbeliever. There is no limit to the number of times we should forgive a brother who errs (Mt. 18:21-22). As Paul wrote,

Do not repay anyone evil for evil. Be careful to do what is right in the eyes of everybody. If it is possible, as far as it depends on you, live at peace with everyone. Do not take revenge, my friends, but leave room for God's wrath, for it is written: "It is mine to avenge; I will repay," says the Lord. On the contrary: "If your enemy is hungry, feed him; if he is thirsty, give him something to drink. In doing this, you will heap burning coals on his head." Do not be overcome by evil, but overcome evil with good (Rom. 12:17-21).

Notice that love for an enemy is mainly a matter of acting right toward him. When we can pass that test of love we are far along the way toward Christian maturity.

Study Questions

1. How does love for God relate to love for others?
2. How can one best express love for God?
3. What are the two greatest biblical passages about love? What is distinctive about each of them?
4. Can you name and discuss two major hindrances to the consistent expression of Christian love?
5. How does Jesus assist us in passing the supreme test of love for enemies?

He Trusts Us
Matthew 10:1-10

The Twelve whom Jesus trusted
To do His work on earth
Were of the ordinary sort
Who seemed of little worth.

In many ways contrasting,
They all declared Him Lord,
And took the big assignment
As preachers of His Word.

They healed the sick, the dead raised,
And served all whom they could,
Looking to the Master
To make them truly good.

They did not serve equally well,
And one our Lord betrayed,
But blessings fell from heaven
Upon the ones who stayed.

And the work that these got started
Is now our work to do.
The task still seems gigantic;
The laborers are few.

Our trust is in Christ Jesus;
His doctrines we discuss,
And yet our minds are startled
That He is trusting us.

— Ed Thiele

CHAPTER 12

SERVANTHOOD

Who does not want to be president of the company instead of just an employee? Who would not prefer being the supervisor instead of the one being supervised? Would anyone rather be the janitor or church secretary than the pastor? In this competitive Western society of ours, it seems like a mistake not to want to be first, at the top of the pyramid, the one in charge, the star. However, Jesus said,

> Not so with you. Instead, whoever wants to become great among you must be your servant, and whoever wants to be first must be slave of all (Mk. 10:43-44).

Was Jesus saying ambition is wrong? Is it more Christian to want to be worst than best, last than first?

We are called to be great servants. Our mission is not to control others but to assist them. We are not to calculate our degree of success as disciples by how many work under us. The goal is service, not success, and the one who can render the best service to the most people is greatest. Ambition is not erased but redirected among Christ's followers.

James and John were wrong to ask Jesus, "Let one of us sit at your right and the other at your left in your glory" (Mk. 10:37). The other ten disciples were mistaken to become indignant with them when they heard about it. Probably they were jealous that they had not thought of it first. All twelve were likely stunned by Jesus' teaching. It runs contrary to human nature to want to excel in serving others, but Jesus lived what He taught and was quite in line with the total biblical revelation.

Biblical Emphases

The term "servant" is found throughout the Bible, and slavery was commonly practiced in the ancient world. The most frequently used Hebrew word is *ebed* meaning a doer, a tiller of the ground, a servant or slave. Besides the expected usage, many leaders are referred to in this way. Moses was "the servant of God."[1] Prophets like Elijah (2 Kg. 9:36), Isaiah (Is. 20:3), and Daniel (Dan. 6:20) were also called God's servants. As king, furthermore, David was called the servant of God (Ps. 78:70); so was the governor of Judah, Zerubbabel (Hag. 2:23); and so were priests who served at God's altar or in His sanctuary (Ezek. 44:11-16). In the Psalms, faithful worshipers are addressed as servants of the Lord (Ps. 113:1; 134:1). Besides these, the nation Israel is repeatedly called "my servant" by God in Isaiah 41, 42, 44, and 49, and the Messiah was foretold to be God's servant (Is. 42:1; 52:13) who would come.

The Greek words in the New Testament which are employed the most to convey this idea are *doulos* meaning servant or slave and *diakonos* translated minister, servant or deacon. Jesus described His role as both master and servant. Although He had all authority as Lord, He said, "I am among you as one who serves" (Lk. 22:27) and "the Son of Man did not come to be served, but to serve, and to give his life as a ransom for many" (Mk. 10:45). Paul described Jesus' humility with the statement that He "made himself nothing, taking the very nature of a servant" (Phil. 2:7). We can never regard it as too humiliating for us to take up the duties and spirit of a servant when we think of our Lord's attitude and example. He not only washed the disciples' feet, He patiently taught them day by day and came to them when they were in trouble. His death for all humanity is, of course, the paramount demonstration of servanthood and the fulfillment of the suffering servant prophesied in Isaiah 53.

Paul was glad to call himself "a servant of Jesus Christ" (Rom. 1:1). Simon Peter, Jude, and James made parallel identifications of themselves to the recipients of their letters.[2] They were claiming no special privileges and seeking no glory for themselves. Neither were they discounting their worth. The description related the truth about who they were and whom they served. Paul stressed a different aspect of the relationship when he wrote, "For we do not preach ourselves, but Jesus Christ as Lord, and ourselves as your servants for Jesus' sake" (2 Cor. 4:5). This is the kind of ministry all of us disciples have received from the Lord. We are His servants and the servants of others for His sake.

"Deacon" is an accurate translation of the word *diakonos* when an

---

[1] 1 Chr. 6:49; 2 Chr. 24:9; Neh. 10:29; Dan. 9:11.
[2] 2 Pet. 1:1; Jude 1; Jas. 1:1.

office in the New Testament church is indicated as in Phil. 1:1 and 1 Tim. 3:8-13. Although the word is not found in Acts 6:1-6, the consensus of Evangelical scholarship is that this is probably the record of the origin of the office, and waiting on tables for equitable food distribution among the widows was the initial assignment. Today, deacons are selected to serve the church in any way they are needed. More often, *diakonos* is translated servant. Even a governing authority is thus "God's servant" to maintain order, punish those who do wrong, and to work for the good of all (Rom. 13:1-6). *Diakonos* can be used, nevertheless, to refer to a minister, one who like Timothy was looking after a church (1 Tim. 4:6). The word *diakonia* is translated both as ministry and service and is used for the work of all God's people (Eph. 4:12) as well as pastoral work like Timothy's (2 Tim. 4:5).

Disciples are all called to be servants. The leaders are to be servants of all who are committed to their care. The idea of a ministry paid to do the work of the church for the church is not discovered in the New Testament.[3] Those who lead are to equip other disciples for their "works of service" (Eph. 4:12). They are not to be dictators, commanders, or bosses. Paul expressed this to the church at Corinth, "Not that we would lord it over your faith, but we work with you for your joy, because it is by faith you stand firm" (2 Cor. 1:24). That is the spirit of a servant-leader. The ideal congregation, on the other hand, is a servant church in which all members are servants of the Lord, of each other, and of the world around them, as far as their energies, resources, and prayers can reach.

Attributes of Good Servants

The attributes of a good servant are not listed in any single biblical passage. Neither is any servant whom we read about in the Scriptures perfect, although there are some good models. Since all Christians are called to be servants and discipleship is closely connected with servanthood, a compilation of some of the valuable traits of a good servant is provided next. The teachings of Jesus are the chief source of these.

Undivided loyalty. The good servant must be absolutely committed

---

[3]The NT teaches that missionaries like Paul and elders like Timothy deserve financial support for their labor (2 Cor. 11:7-9; 1 Tim. 5:17-18).

to his Lord. Jesus said,

> No servant can serve two masters. Either he will hate the one and love the other, or he will be devoted to the one and despise the other. You cannot serve both God and Money (Lk. 16:13).

The servant of the Lord should establish unrivaled allegiance to Jesus Christ.[4] Discipleship is a total life commitment. Money is not the only challenger. Power and pleasure are two others which can be quickly named. Jesus mentioned family as another competitor for first place, and He remarked, "If anyone comes to me and does not hate his father and mother, his wife and children, his brothers and sisters—yes, even his own life—he cannot be my disciple" (Lk.14:26). Of course, Jesus did not mean for us to hate them in the sense of intense rejection and hostility, but to be so devoted to Him that all other attachments are clearly secondary.

Subordination. The good servant must be under the orders of his superior. One must stay ready to obey. Jesus taught the disciples,

> A student is not above his teacher, nor a servant above his master. It is enough for the student to be like his teacher and the servant like his master (Mt. 10:24-25).

Disciples must not run ahead of the Lord or proceed presumptuously without consulting Him. Our charge is not to create a new pattern but to follow His. Conformity to Christ will often make us non-conformists in a pagan culture.

Obedience. The chief duty of a servant is obedience. In order to be good servants, Christians must know and do what our Master has commanded us to do. The New Testament has many imperative verbs such as "go," "pray," "give," "preach," and many others. We should look for these orders and for ways to carry them out. The centurion who sought healing for his servant from Jesus understood this. He said,

> For I myself am a man under authority, with soldiers under me. I tell this one, "Go," and he goes; and that one "Come," and he comes. I say to my servant, "Do this," and he does it (Mt. 8:9).

---

[4]See the full discussion in Chapter 2, "Living Under His Lordship."

So the centurion simply asked Jesus to issue the command for healing and he believed it would happen. Christ should be obeyed without our expecting thanks from Him. He put that teaching in a servant parable and concluded by saying, "So you also, when you have done everything you were told to do, should say, 'We are unworthy servants; we have only done our duty'" (Lk. 17:10). Are you willing to serve without recognition or applause?

Commitment to Service. The word for servant has "serve" in it. Why is it that some believers find the word servant applied to themselves so repulsive, so degrading? Someone has said, "Service is the rent we pay for the space we occupy." Ours is a much greater incentive for wanting to be committed to service than paying rent. We have been greatly served by the Lord who has called us to serve others as He has served us. In sending out the Twelve, He instructed them,

> As you go, preach this message; "The kingdom of heaven is near." Heal the sick, raise the dead, cleanse those who have leprosy, drive out demons. Freely you have received, freely give (Mt. 10:7-8).

With the same authority Jesus gave them to work miracles in His name, we are to be committed to service, helping others in every way possible. Never in our country's history have the churches and community agencies been so dependent on volunteers to sustain the programs of service they project as they are now. Christians should be in the majority among such volunteers.

Generosity. Being generous with money, possessions, time, and effort should be characteristic of good servants. The good servant surrenders rights of ownership gladly to meet the needs of others. Most opportunities of service require some sacrifice. Jesus told the disciples, "Sell your possessions and give to the poor" (Lk. 12:33), and "Any of you who does not give up everything he has cannot be my disciple" (Lk. 14:33). Also, He called the attention of His disciples to the sacrifice of a poor widow who gave into the temple treasury two small coins, all she had. Good servants will reveal the generosity that is seen in the One whom they serve who gave His all.

Courage. The attribute of courage should also be demonstrated in the decisions of good servants. Jesus never minimized the difficulties to be endured by His followers. He frequently warned of dangers and opposition that they would face, but added encouragement. He said, "I tell you, my friends, do not be afraid of those who kill the body and after that can do no more" (Lk. 12:4). Also, when they were put on trial before various authorities, they were to depend on the Holy Spirit to teach them how to respond (Lk. 12:11-12). Instead of fearing how they would survive, their faith should inspire bravery. Jesus remarked, "Do not be afraid, little flock, for your Father has been pleased to give you the kingdom" (Lk. 12:32). The way of a devoted servant of the Lord is still not easy, but courage inspired by the Spirit's presence and the Father's loving care can enable one to meet each stressful situation that arises.

Preparation. The final attribute of a good servant on my list is preparation. The parables which Jesus used with His disciples to help them prepare for judgment and for His glorious return were mostly servant parables. They stressed readiness, watchfulness, and preparation. The parable of the talents (Mt. 25:14-30) and the one about the owner of the house leaving one servant-manager in charge of the other servants (Mt. 24:45-51; Mk. 13:34-37; Lk. 12:42-48) are primary examples. "Be dressed, ready for service and keep your lamps burning" (Lk. 12:35) are the words of our Lord which reveal the main emphasis of this teaching. As His servants, we are to be busy doing what He assigned us to do with an eager readiness for His return. "For the Son of Man is going to come in his Father's glory with his angels, and then he will reward each person according to what he has done" (Mt. 16:27).

Lessons for Christian Slaves

Slavery was very common in the Roman world of New Testament times. As T. R. Glover pointed out, "There were different types of slavery in the ancient world."[5] One's secretary, or teacher, or friend might be a slave. The concept of redemption comes from the purchase of a slave for the purpose of setting him or her free. A sizable number of those becoming spiritually redeemed through Christ were slaves. Paul wrote,

Brothers, think of what you were when you were called. Not many of you were wise by human standards; not many were influential; not many were of noble birth (1 Cor. 1:26).

---

[5]T. R. Glover, *The Disciple* (Cambridge: The University Press, 1942), 13.

One of the problems Paul faced in the young churches was the lack of real spiritual unity in congregations made up of both slaves and free (Gal. 3:26-28). Also the Apostle wrote to Philemon about welcoming back his runaway slave Onesimus who by being saved had become "a dear brother" and "useful" (Phil. 1:15-16, 11).

Therefore, in Paul's letters to the Ephesians and the Colossians, he addressed some words specifically to the slave members of those and other churches. Many of us can apply these to ourselves as employees who work with accountability to others. All of us, however, are called to be servants or slaves of the Lord and we certainly can see the relevance of these lessons to our lives.

First, remember who owns us. Just as slaves never forgot who their owners were, we need that awareness of belonging to Christ. He purchased us for Himself by laying down His life for us (1 Cor. 6:19-20). Thus, Paul wrote, "It is the Lord Christ you are serving" (Col. 3:24). A natural consequence should be a change of affections. "Those who belong to Christ Jesus have crucified the sinful nature with its passions and desires" (Gal. 5:24). Servanthood is linked to that sense of His ownership of our lives.

Second, we are to obey Him with reverence and sincerity. Besides obedience being important, the attitude with which we obey is also significant. Look at the way the exhortation is written:

Slaves, obey your earthly masters with respect and fear, and with sincerity of heart, just as you would obey Christ. Obey them not only to win their favor when their eye is on you, but like slaves of Christ, doing the will of God from your heart (Eph. 6:5-6).

With a proper feeling of His right as Lord to control us and a genuine delight in being allowed to serve such a gracious Master, we should endeavor to show our love for Him by keeping His commands (Jn. 14:21).

Third, we learn from the biblical admonition to Christian slaves that we are to serve enthusiastically. In almost identical words, Paul directed this instruction to the slaves at Ephesus and at Colossae: they were to serve their earthly masters like they were to serve the Lord, "whole-heartedly" (Eph. 6:7-8; Col. 3:23-24). A generous reward is assured, "an inheritance," since both the conversion and the calling are by the grace of God (Acts 20:32). Ordinarily, a slave would have no inheritance, but in God's family slaves have full benefits.

Ways to Serve

Many ways for serving the Lord are available. There are as many ways as there are people and their needs. While disciples are uniquely equipped to assist others in meeting their spiritual needs, they are expected to respond compassionately to others' physical needs too. Jesus made it clear that supplying food, clothing, and medical care to persons who lack these is considered service offered to Him. One way we can aid those we meet is to treat them with courtesy. Paul stated, "Therefore, as we have opportunity, let us do good to all people, especially to those who belong to the family of believers" (Gal. 6:10).[6] Using our homes to provide hospitality is another basic sort of service. Jesus urged us not to invite only those who can return the favor, but to share the food and fellowship of our homes with the disadvantaged. He said, "When you give a banquet, invite the poor, the crippled, the lame, the blind, and you will be blessed" (Lk. 14:13). Besides being a specific directive, that teaching of Jesus should challenge us to seek out persons with many kinds of needs to whom we can minister in many ways. Internationals in our country have language and culture problems. Aged persons may require transportation, shopping assistance, and telephone calls for security. Let's use our eyes, our ears, and our imaginations to discover needs that we and our churches may provide.

Study Questions

1. How is the term servant used throughout the Scriptures?
2. Can you name the attributes of a good servant as gathered from several different locations in the Scriptures?
3. What lessons for life discipleship can you draw from the biblical teachings directed to Christian slaves?

---

[6]Cf. Tit. 3:1-2.

CHAPTER 13

DISCIPLEMAKING

The subject of disciplemaking has been reserved for this location in the book to stress its relation to all that has gone before in the discussion. Being a disciple precedes making disciples. The heart should be right; Christ's lordship should be accepted; godliness should be our goal; and the disciplines should be practiced as we are seeking to communicate our beliefs and lead others to embrace them. We have just been thinking about servanthood, and clearly the highest service a disciple ever renders to another individual is to facilitate that person's salvation through faith in Jesus Christ. We are ready to consider our evangelistic privilege and responsibility.

Fruitful discipleship includes witnessing to others of our trust in Jesus and of His desire to save them from their sins and to give them eternal life. Paul wrote to the Roman Christians expressing his hope to share in their harvest by leading Gentiles in that imperial city to be saved (Rom. 1:13). He had a feeling of obligation to share the gospel and an eagerness to make Christ known. He wrote, "I am not ashamed of the gospel, because it is the power of God for the salvation of everyone who believes" (Rom. 1:16). Paul's remarkable experiences of observing the power of the gospel in many places are familiar to us from readings in Acts. Even imprisonment provided openings to tell the good news about his Lord (Acts 16:25-34). Trials before rulers gave him chances to deliver his testimony (Acts 26:1-32). Everywhere he went he was an ambassador for Christ. Paul is a superb example of fruitful discipleship. All did not believe, but many did. The more we tell the unsaved about our Lord, the more fruitfulness we may expect.

The Greek word translated "to make disciples" is *matheteuo*. The verb is used twice in the New Testament, in the imperative *matheteusate* of Mt. 28:19 and in the past participle, *matheteusantes*, "having made disciples," in Acts 14:21. Just as a *mathetes* (disciple) is more than a learner, to make disciples is to do more than teach.[1] What our commission states in Mt. 28:19-20 is that all disciples are to make disciples, baptizing and teaching them to obey all that Jesus commanded. Disciplemaking is evangelism which incorporates baptism, nurture, and

---

[1]See the discussion of *mathetes* in Chapter One.

instruction as vital parts of helping disciples express and grow in their commitment to Jesus Christ as Savior and Lord.

To make a disciple is, first of all, to share the gospel with another person whom the Holy Spirit convicts of sin and the need to trust Christ for salvation. When another person is won to faith in Jesus and willingness to follow Him, a disciple is made. Seldom is a single conversion the result of only one Christian's witness. More often numerous believers over an extended period of time share the message about Jesus until the invitation to receive Him is acted upon by the unbeliever in a positive response. So, making disciples is something we do together even if only one witness is able to see the conversion occur. Furthermore, several Christians should be involved in affirming the new convert in the way of Christ.

Jesus' Call to Discipleship

When Jesus called the fishermen to follow Him, He also called them to work with Him in making disciples. "'Come, follow me,' Jesus said, 'and I will make you fishers of men'" (Mt. 4:19). How much they understood we do not know, but what He had in mind is clear to us. They were to lead in a movement which would "catch" people to be His committed followers. The ones caught would be taught, trained, and empowered to continue the disciplemaking. Jesus does not grade disciples to decide which ones may participate in this endeavor. He calls every disciple to make disciples, and each one qualifies by reporting for duty.

Andrew caught on in a hurry. Look at the narrative:

The first thing Andrew did was to find his brother Simon and tell him, "We have found the Messiah" (that is, the Christ). And he brought him to Jesus (Jn. 1:41-42).

Philip, likewise, who was from the same town as Andrew and Simon, discovered Jesus to be the promised one and invited Nathanael to meet Him (Jn. 1:43-46). Matthew grasped that aspect of his Master's call. He showed that he did by following Jesus and serving dinner at his house for the Lord and some disciples to meet a bunch of his cronies who were "sinners" (Mt. 9:9-13). That is the way the Master's plan is supposed to work. Jesus summons sinners to salvation, discipleship, and disciplemaking. There are not three separate calls. One of the best times for a disciple to bring others to Jesus is immediately after one's conversion.

A New Life Foundation

Witnessing to others about Jesus and salvation begins with the evidence of a change in the life of one or more believers. New life observed in Jesus' followers forms the foundation for the verbal witness, supplying an effective visual aid. A Christian life of love and goodness alone will not save anyone, but the living of such a life produces credibility among hearers of the gospel. Many people would be willing to put their faith in Jesus if they could be convinced that sinful lives can really be changed. Paul's exhortations sometimes sounded like this:

> Let us put aside the deeds of darkness and put on the armor of light (Rom. 13:12).

> You were taught, with regard to your former way of life, to put off your old self, which is being corrupted by its deceitful desires; to be made new in the attitude of your minds; and to put on the new self, created to be like God in true righteousness and holiness (Eph. 4:22-24).

Paul was urging churches to realize that every member must strive to be living proof of Jesus' ability to make life new from the inside out. A better quality of ethical behavior is persuasive.

This does not mean that one has to be living almost perfectly before being able to speak to another about Jesus. Any Christian can tell about the wonderful new life Christ brings, while honestly admitting personal short-comings. Normally a believer can relate better to the unconverted when confessing that inward struggles against temptation continue after one is saved. This is a good way to project the truth that we are saved by God's grace not by our goodness and that growth should continue throughout one's life.

Comprehending that all are called to disciplemaking is a great incentive for each disciple to maintain a disciplined life. The freshness and vitality which we expect of a new convert may be sustained in the maturing life. The secret is simply living in the presence of God, walking in step with the Spirit, and being obedient to our Lord. The finest Christians I have known always seemed as though they had just been talking with the Lord, receiving their guidance from Him. They were witnessing by the nature of their redeemed personalities. This is what Paul was appealing for when he wrote,

> Do everything without complaining or arguing, so that you may become blameless and pure, children of God without fault in a crooked and depraved generation, in which you shine like stars in the universe as you hold out the word of life (Phil. 2:14-16).

If we are going to be used by God in declaring the message that leads others to discipleship, we should try to stay so close to the Lord that our new life is a foundation for our words about what Jesus can do for sinners.

By Love Compelled

The best motivation for disciplemaking is Christian love. Any unselfish contemplation of the plight of perishing sinners should prompt a believer to tell them the good news of the Savior. Paul was driven in his evangelism by this compassionate concern. When he was not preaching to them, he was praying for them (1 Cor. 9:16, 19-23; Rom. 10:1). He said, "For Christ's love compels us, because we are convinced that one died for all, and therefore all died" (2 Cor. 5:14). His compulsion to evangelize stemmed from his encounter with the loving Savior who died for everybody. If Jesus would suffer on the cross to save sinners, surely, Paul felt, the apostle could spend his life relating to others these truths about Him that could change their lives and their relationship to God forever.

Whatever you can do to keep the thought of Christ's love for you and for all humanity prominent in your thinking, do it. Memorize Scriptures and hymns about it, read about it, talk about it, sing about it. Nothing else moves us to seek to rescue the perishing like the keen awareness of Jesus' desire to save sinners which led Him to lay down His life for wayward sheep.[2] When you pray for unsaved friends, recall how much the Lord loves them.

Various factors have motivated Christians to attempt to make disciples. Guilt has been used often to induce Christians to witness.

---

[2]See Mt. 9:36; Jn. 10:11; Is. 53:6.

Recognition and reward have also stimulated some to share their faith. Employment at churches and church-related agencies or holding an unpaid leadership position has obligated some to practice evangelism. Those, however, who are compelled by love, Christ's love for all and their love for Christ and for others, obviously have the superior motivation.

Practical Procedures

Since disciplemaking deserves a high priority in a disciple's life, I want to be as practical as possible in assisting disciples to be consistent in trying to win others. The procedures I suggest are as follows:

1. **Keep a prayer list** of specific persons who do not appear to be disciples of Christ and pray for them regularly.
2. **Polish your testimony.** Write it out so it can be spoken briefly and effectively. Eliminate words that do not communicate clearly to an unchurched person. Make it interesting and doctrinally sound.
3. **Cultivate a friendly disposition.** Practice starting a conversation with strangers and showing sincere interest in others. Ask non-threatening questions.
4. **Learn to turn the conversation to spiritual subjects.** Donald S. Whitney recommends asking the person how you can pray for him or her.[3] Very often the opening will emerge easily.[4]
5. **Have a plan for presenting the gospel.** Memorize useful Scripture verses or at least the biblical references so that you may read them. Even though you want to be relaxed and natural, a plan will help you to be briefer without omitting any essential truth.[5]
6. **Be sensitive** to the interest level and reactions of the person to whom you are speaking. It is usually not wise to proceed if one is not showing favorable interest. Also, you may sense that one has questions which need answering before you continue.
7. **Know how to invite others to receive Jesus Christ** and salvation

---

[3]Donald S. Whitney, *Spiritual Disciplines for the Christian Life* (Colorado Springs: NavPress, 1991), 103. See the entire Chapter 6, "Evangelism," for further suggestions.

[4]Study Jesus' conversation with the woman of Samaria in Jn. 4:4-26.

[5]C.W.T. (Continuous Witness Training) offers one such plan for a thorough gospel presentation and training for its use.

through faith in Him. Be sure they understand what to do and what Christ has promised to do for them. Assist them as necessary in praying a simple prayer requesting forgiveness and expressing faith in the Lord.

Much has been written about personal evangelism.[6] You will want to keep preparing for your task in disciplemaking throughout your life by study and experience. In this brief discussion I have touched on only a few practical procedures that have been important for me.

Various Types of Witnessing

Persons can be led to repent of their sins, place their faith in Jesus as Savior and surrender to Him as Lord using various types of witnessing. The message is the same, but the methods may differ.

One type of witnessing is done **at the church building** during regular times of meeting. It is a team effort. The pastor occasionally preaches evangelistic sermons and often explains how an individual becomes a Christian. Bible teachers teach and include information about conversion, particularly when they are aware of a lost person being present. Musicians witness by exalting the Savior in the songs that are sung and played. Printed materials which are distributed may state how an individual can be saved. All the faithful members participate in the witness that is made to the unconverted by attending when church is assembled for study and worship.

Another type of witnessing is **systematic visitation**. A witness is made at the home of the evangelistic prospect either by appointment or without it. The visitor may have only the name and address of a person who is unchurched with the assignment to make the contact, or the one without Christ may have attended the church or otherwise have indicated interest so that a visitor with some acquaintance with the person can be sent. Many have been won to Christ in the privacy of their own homes by the assigned visit of a Christian witness.

Spontaneous witnessing also sometimes results in salvation. The unanticipated opportunity to help another find Christ may occur on an airplane trip, or at a garage while an automobile is being repaired. Anywhere that a Christian and a non-Christian are together long enough

---

[6]See selected bibliography at the end of the book for recommendations.

to have a personal conversation could result in a witness being given.

A fourth type is **relational witnessing**.[7] One or both parents may gently lead a child to trust in Jesus for eternal life. A wife may prayerfully help her husband to know Jesus in His saving power. All the relationships of family and friends afford avenues for conversing about spiritual truth. Every person with whom we already have a good relationship, if unsaved, could be one whom God would reconcile to Himself using our witness. The repetitive contact with such persons makes it possible for us to plant the seed and cultivate it gradually.

Witnessing through a public worship service, systematic visitation by assignment, spontaneous sharing of the good news in casual contacts and sustained witnessing to family members and friends are the best ways I know. A periodic review of these different types of witnessing with a prayer that God will allow us to witness in all of these ways could make us more fruitful disciplemakers.

A Power Pact

Every disciple tends to wonder if he or she has what it takes to witness about Christ. Could we really be instrumental in changing the life and destiny of another person? Could we say something that would open the very door of heaven for someone? If we are truly disciples of Jesus, surely we can influence others positively toward making a faith commitment of themselves to Christ. Just as He alone can save, He alone can enable us to be effective witnesses.

We who endeavor to communicate the gospel have Jesus' promise of power. We might call it a power pact He has made with us. He said, "You will receive power when the Holy Spirit comes on you; and you will be my witnesses in Jerusalem, and in all Judea and Samaria, and to the ends of the earth" (Acts 1:8). The Holy Spirit has now been given to all believers and will be given to all who trust Christ in the future. When the first disciples at Jerusalem experienced the coming of the Spirit upon them, Peter proclaimed to all who would believe, "You will receive the gift of the Holy Spirit. The promise is for you and your children and for all who are far off—for all whom the Lord our God will call" (Acts 2:38-39). The Holy Spirit supplies the power of God working in us and

---

[7]See Oscar Thompson, *Concentric Circles of Concern*, for an excellent treatment of relational witnessing.

through us as we live and speak for Jesus.

How can we know that we have the Spirit's power as we try to make disciples? Feelings are not the proof of the presence of the Spirit with us, feelings either in ourselves or the person(s) to whom we witness. Results are not the reliable gauge either. Witnessing in the power of the Spirit does not guarantee that the lost person receiving the witness will be converted. If the unsaved person is convicted of guilt in regard to sin, that is the work of the Spirit (Jn. 16:8); and if the individual is saved, that is clearly the work of the Spirit too (Jn. 3:5-6; Tit. 3:5-6). Otherwise, we claim the promise of Jesus by faith alone that when we witness of Him we have the power of the Holy Spirit. In Acts the reader sees example after example of the promise being fulfilled.[8] The story of churches being started and of the number of disciples increasing greatly is the story of the Spirit at work in disciples for the mission of disciple-making. The story is continuing today and we can decide to put ourselves in the story.

Overcoming Fear

The biggest barrier that most of us face in attempting to serve as witnesses of Christ is fear. Strong men and confident women often wilt before the challenge of talking about Jesus Christ to other people. It is not only speaking to strangers about such a personal matter as one's relationship to God that intimidates us. We may find even that easier than speaking of this to a close friend or relative. Let's face it, rarely do we bring up the subject of faith in Christ without some fear.

What are we afraid of? Have you heard of anyone lately who was attacked and killed by a resentful lost person with whom the victim had attempted to share a Christian testimony? Violent persecution or opposition is not the major deterrent to witnessing. Fear of failure and rejection is the major problem for sincere Christians. Such fear is not a bad thing unless we give in to it. Fear is for overcoming. Faith grows whenever we surmount this barrier. Joseph of Arimathea had kept his discipleship a secret "for fear of the Jews" (Jn. 19:38) until after Jesus was crucified. But he came forward to ask Pilate for the privilege of burying Jesus' body and completed that action at considerable risk. His faith and courage are memorable.

---

[8]See Acts 4:31, 33; 5:42; 8:4, 26-39; 9:31.

The joy of involvement in giving the witness by which a condemned sinner is saved is possible only if the fear of a negative reaction is conquered. The writer of Hebrews reminds us to say with confidence, "The Lord is my helper; I will not be afraid. What can man do to me?" (Heb. 13:6). We can know the applicability of Paul's encouragement to Timothy,

> For God did not give us a spirit of timidity, but a spirit of power, of love and of self-discipline. So do not be ashamed to testify about our Lord (2 Tim. 1:7-8).

Could we be ashamed of Jesus, of who He is, of what He has done for us? It seems impossible, but all who have tried to share their faith know the reality of fear. Fruitfulness accompanies faithfulness. Jesus said, "Be faithful, even to the point of death, and I will give you the crown of life" (Rev. 2:10). Fearfulness threatens to rob us of many blessings, but it can be overcome.

Nurturing the Newborn

Initial commitment of a person to Jesus is the starting point of discipleship. What happens immediately after that significantly determines the quality of the rest of that Christian's life. Post-natal care of the newborn is vital. Nurture is necessary for growth.

Nurture for the newborn Christian should consist of loving attention and spiritual food. The one who first talks to the new believer after conversion begins the process by helping to clarify and affirm the decision. Counseling at this time should be centered on assurance that the person has believed in Christ for salvation and voluntarily surrendered to Him to begin to live as a Christian. In most cases, the person who has helped the convert to make this decision is the ideal person to offer the assistance, but any Christian might be trained to do so.

Some recommended verses for use in assurance of salvation are these: 1 Jn. 5:11-13; Jn. 10:27-29; Eph. 2:8-9; Rom. 10:9-10, 13, and Heb. 7:25. At least one or more of these should be read and discussed with the new Christian.

An explanation of the importance of a daily quiet time of Bible reading and prayer should be given. Suggest that one of the Gospels is usually the best place to begin reading. Tell the person why this practice of personal worship is so valuable. Someone should talk about baptism and church affiliation with the individual. Describe the schedule and procedure in your church if that is likely to be the church of choice by the newborn. Help him or her to anticipate reception by the church. The significance of Bible teaching, preaching, and public worship should be emphasized. Introduce the believer to church members and advise forming friendships with several more mature members.

The process of nurturing the newborn is assigned to the whole church, but specific members should be charged with responsibility for doing this. They may be called sponsors, encouragers or something else. A new members' class may be offered. A membership committee may supervise the assimilation of new members. Some excellent materials are available for enabling a new Christian to be well-established in the first stage of discipleship.[9]

No attempt is being made to list all that should be covered in the nurturing phase. This may vary from person to person and church to church. The length of the phase may also be flexible, but at least the first six weeks after conversion are crucial and six months is not too long for follow-up. We must do a better job of nurturing the "child of God."

Discipleship Continues

The follow-up phase is only the first stage of discipleship. Discipleship is a lifelong process. Every disciple needs help from other Christians throughout life. The goal, however, is for each disciple to require less personal assistance from others as the maturation progresses. The building of a life pattern that centers in the personal relationship with Christ takes time. Stability and strength are rooted in habits that must be formed and maintained. Christians who have demonstrated growth and maturity can offer valuable aid to disciples who are younger in the faith.

The beginning of a discipling relationship may originate at either end. The newer Christian may arrange to meet with a respected more mature disciple or the latter may take the initiative in offering to meet with the former. A time and place are sufficient to get started. The number and

---

[9]Ralph W. Neighbour, Jr., *Survival Kit for New Christians, I* (Nashville: Convention Press, 1979); Waylon B. Moore, *New Testament Follow-Up* (Grand Rapids, MI: Eerdmans, 1963); Gary W. Kuhne, *The Dynamics of Personal Follow-Up* (Grand Rapids, MI: Zondervan, 1978).

frequency of meetings can be mutually agreed upon. No particular structure is required. Probably the focus will be on felt needs or problems in the life of the newer Christian. Free, confidential discussion and prayer are the keys. Bible study or book study may be included. Friendship built around Jesus Christ and commitment to Him as Lord is the nature of such discipling.[10]

Unfortunately, many Christians have become disgruntled drop-outs because of personal problems and crises they did not know how to cope with. Instead of seeking help from a more mature Christian, they gave up in disgust. Or perhaps they sought help, but no one trained to assist them responded. Too many disciples have been dropped too soon after conversion. When trouble came, they did not know what to do. Problems can be instrumental in the formation of Christian maturity if properly met with resilient faith.

Discipling others can be done in groups as well as one-on-one. Jesus showed us how by facilitating the growth of a group as well as assisting with problems and needs of individual members of the group. An additional benefit of group discipleship training is that group members can support and assist one another. Already existing groups, such as ongoing Bible classes, can also serve as discipleship training groups if they are person-centered and not just content-centered. Excellent materials are available for discipleship training groups to use that combine Bible study with life application. A leader who is personally committed to growth toward maturity is essential to the effectiveness of such groups.

The presence of a group of maturing disciples who are sharing their faith in Christ with the unsaved and with newer Christians is the best indication that the discipleship program of Jesus is being followed. The commission to make disciples is carried out by witnessing, nurturing the newborn, and training disciples. When the converted are seeking to be instrumental in the conversion of the lost and the spiritual growth of other believers while still pursuing their own growth, they are following Christ's plan. This is a plan for all His people in all nations until His final coming.

The emphasis I have tried to make throughout this book is that every disciple is accountable for his or her own spiritual growth and fruitfulness. Desire, disciplines, and cooperation must come from the heart of each disciple. No external authority or force can make discipleship

---

[10]Spiritual direction is a phrase sometimes used to describe this discipling ministry.

development occur. Nevertheless, the church, church leaders, and other disciples can and should help each convert to grow if given the opportunity to assist. Bringing every believer to full maturity in Christ is the ultimate goal.

Study Questions

1. How is disciplemaking related to personal evangelism?
2. What part does the changed life of the Christian play in the effectiveness of the verbal witness?
3. What are some ways we can keep ourselves motivated to witness from love for the lost?
4. Can you mention four types of witnessing?
5. Are you able to describe some helpful steps in nurturing a newborn Christian?
6. Will you compare the benefits of one-on-one and group discipling?

CHAPTER 14

VICTORY IN SPIRITUAL WARFARE

As long as I can remember I have enjoyed singing "Onward, Christian Soldiers." A rousing, marching song like that stirs the heart and prepares one for action. As a child, however, I would soon calm down and go to sleep as the preacher began to preach. It was years later before I was able to relate the message of that song to my own spiritual warfare. The church's response to the "call to war" is not much better than my childlike one. We do not take very seriously God's command to prepare for spiritual warfare and to move forward to claim spiritual victory.

The great passage on spiritual warfare in Eph. 6:10-18 is the final lesson addressed to the church in Ephesus. Probably a circuit of churches in Asia Minor received this exhortation after the Ephesian church did. The message is for all Christians. Spiritual warfare continues. The metaphor of a battle will always fit the circumstances of disciples living in a sinful world.

Jesus never promised His followers that discipleship would be easy. Before sending the Twelve out on their first mission in Galilee, He warned them that rejection, hatred, arrest and trial would come. He also assured them of God's care and vindication. Although they were like "sheep among wolves" (Mt. 10:16), they had a good Shepherd. They would ultimately be rewarded. Jesus did not call His disciples soldiers, but He did use the warfare image in His parable on counting the cost. A king would surely assess the number of fighting men his enemy possessed in comparison to his own troops before going into battle against them, He said (Lk. 14:31-33). Jesus had counted the cost of winning the victory against Satan and was prepared to pay that cost. He wanted His followers to be ready to fight against evil also.

Roman soldiers were everywhere in the first century world. Paul used an analogy that was familiar to his readers. He may very well have been chained to a Roman guard at the time he wrote the letter to the church at Ephesus. Those who had hoped that Jesus would lead a revolt to overthrow Rome or at least drive the Roman armies out of Palestine now needed to have their vision reframed. Paul told how a much more important and lasting victory may be won.

The Nature of Our Warfare

"Our struggle," Paul wrote, "is not against flesh and blood, but against the rulers, against the authorities, against the powers of this dark world and against the spiritual forces of evil in the heavenly realms" (Eph. 6:12). The warfare is not against other people, but that does not mean it is any less real. The fighting is spiritual. The battlefield is primarily within. The conflict is over interior territory that is rightfully the property of God. Jesus spoke of the heart as the source of both good and evil (Mk. 7:14-23).[1] It was Satan filling the heart of Annanias that caused him to deceive the church and lie to the Holy Spirit (Acts 5:3). An invisible battle goes on frequently within us as we make choices. We are aware of our consciences, and we know that this inner sense of right or wrong plays a part in our decisions. Previous experiences of pain or satisfaction also are a factor in determining what we will do. Others' expectations of us influence our course of action. Fear of the consequences of wrongdoing may push us toward acceptable behavior. Nevertheless, we think, feel, speak, and act wrongly sometimes, and when we do we understand we have lost a battle in spiritual warfare.

By stressing *spiritual* warfare, then, we are just emphasizing the fact that the Christian's struggle to make good decisions is not primarily a matter of native intelligence or physical vitality. The nature of the conflict is deeper. For the Christian, the Spirit of God living within and desiring control for the sake of Jesus is being contested. The believer will either yield to the Spirit's guidance and resist Satan or resist the Spirit's leadership and submit to Satan. One's choice is free, and it matters immensely. One of the most important aspects of fruitful discipleship is developing skill through the Spirit at winning battles in spiritual warfare.

Confronting the Enemy

Many in modern times have rejected belief in the devil. They have decided that such a concept is unsophisticated. The academician C. S. Lewis, however, wrote, "There are two equal and opposite errors into which our race can fall about the devils. One is to disbelieve in their existence. The other is to believe, and to feel an excessive and unhealthy

---

[1]See Chapter 6, "The Heart of Discipleship."

interest in them."[2] Those two errors continue to be observed. Satan wants humanity to overestimate him or underestimate him.

The Bible teaches us that a personal devil exists, that he is the enemy of God and of persons made in the image of God. He is called Satan, which may mean hater, accuser, adversary, an opposing spirit. "Demon" and the plural, "demons," is found in Mt. 9:34 and is a transliteration of *daimon* instead of a translation. The term "devil" in the Greek, *diabolos*, means the accuser or slanderer. These words reveal some features of our enemy—"the evil one" (Mt. 6:13). He hates, accuses, tempts, and slanders people.

Also the devil's activity is described as being like a hungry lion (1 Pet. 5:8), an old serpent (Rev. 12:9; 20:2), an oppressor (Acts 10:38), and a dragon (Rev. 20:2). In teaching about judgment, Jesus said the eternal fire was "prepared for the devil and his angels" (Mt. 25:41). However, in the Ephesians 6 passage the stratagems of the devil are described as "schemes" (Eph. 6:11) and his use of flaming arrows is mentioned (Eph. 6:16). The chief work of Satan is to tempt people to sin. This is how we are introduced to him biblically (Gen. 3:1-15). Jesus was tempted by him in the desert at the beginning of His ministry. Matthew and Luke both recorded the conflict in vivid detail (Mt. 4:1-11 and Lk. 4:1-13). The devil is the tempter of all humanity (1 Cor. 10:13). No doubt you have met him in that capacity, as I have.

Satan is opposed to God. He has nothing in common with God and is fighting against all of God's purposes for humanity. He is an enemy of every church and of every disciple who is trying to do the will of God. Although he cannot cause a saved person to be lost again, he can work to destroy any useful witness or Christian influence which a believer might have. He would like to keep every unsaved person lost and every saved person in bondage to his old sinful nature so as not to bring any glory to the Savior.

Several battle areas in which the devil is known to attack are these:

1. **Physical**. By sickness or suffering he may weaken the faith and hope of a believer. By enticing to gluttony, drunkenness, smoking, and use of addictive drugs, Satan may gain dominance over a person's life and reduce that one to spiritual impotence.
2. **Moral**. Satan will tempt a person to steal, lie, kill, and indulge in

---

[2]C. S. Lewis, *The Screwtape Letters* (New York: Macmillan, 1943), 9.

sexual or other kinds of immorality.
3. **Spiritual.** The devil wants to popularize any form of idolatry and allegiance to false gods. He entices persons to be caught up in selfish desires and pleasures. He attempts to draw disciples away from enthusiastic commitment to Jesus Christ as Lord.
4. **Theological.** All kinds of heresies, cult teachings, and doubts are promoted by the evil one who wants to keep individuals in darkness concerning God, Jesus, and the Holy Spirit—three in unity. Satan hates the truth.
5. **Psychological.** Satan also desires to keep a person plagued with superstition, fear, guilt, depression, and worry. He seeks mind control.

This list of five battle areas is presented only to help us to be conscious of the breadth of Satan's attack plans. The goal is for us to be able to say as Paul did regarding Satan, "We are not unaware of his schemes" (2 Cor. 2:11). The biblical revelation enables us to confront our enemy realistically.

Strategies of Satan

Ancient warfare was characterized by several different military strategies. Although weaponry has been greatly modified since then, combat on land involves the same basic strategies today. These may be described as (1) a frontal assault, (2) a siege or blockade, (3) ambush, (4) invasion and occupation, and (5) infiltration.

Satan uses these same strategies in spiritual warfare. The direct solicitation to practice evil is a frontal assault. We are all vulnerable in spots. He knows our weaknesses. As James wrote, "each one is tempted when, by his own evil desire, he is dragged away and enticed" (Jas. 1:14). The temptation to Adam and Eve was in the form of an attractive proposition offered in opposition to God's command. The temptations of Jesus were similar. Sometimes we are tempted like that.

When a person is isolated from the normal, spiritual support system, Satan may seem to encircle the individual and take advantage of the weakened position. A young person in college, in military service, or working away from home may be assaulted by the devil and may succumb more easily to temptation then. The disciple without relation to a Christian community is also blockaded by the enemy. Satan can handle us better if we are separated from fellow believers.

The devil also likes to attack us when we least expect it. As a preacher, I have been ambushed right after leading in a successful revival or a fund-raising endeavor. Proud and relaxed, with spiritual defenses down, I have met Satan when I was not prepared for combat. The adversary likes to attack when we are preoccupied with material concerns or personal prestige.

The analogy of invasion and occupation as a strategy of Satan emphasizes the attack and control method. Addiction to drugs, alcohol, and nicotine may serve as examples. One's entire life can be held in the grip of a vice that seemed not serious when the person yielded to an initial temptation of self-abuse. A deep mental depression or a long physical illness may also represent a Satanic occupation in some cases. Demon possession was this type of strategy. The disciple is wise to resist the enemy with all one's strength and the power of the Spirit at the point of invasion.

Infiltration is also a strategy Satan uses. He likes to work through people close to us whom we perceive to be on our side. Jesus understood that this was happening when Peter tried to steer Him away from going to Jerusalem to suffer and die. Well-meaning Peter was rebuked when the Lord said,

> Get behind me, Satan! You are a stumbling block to me; you do not have in mind the things of God, but the things of men (Mt. 16:23).

Moreover, one reason that expulsion of an offending member from the fellowship must remain a valid alternative for a church is that Satan can use even one person to hinder the witness of the whole congregation. As an old maxim states, "One bad apple spoils the barrel." Paul advised the Corinthian church concerning a member charged with sexual immorality, "Hand this man over to Satan" (1 Cor. 5:5). This stern action of excommunication was intended to correct and restore the offender through repentance and to halt this work of Satan in that church.

This discussion of Satan's strategies is intended to be suggestive, not exhaustive. Our spiritual adversary is clever and subtle. That is the main truth communicated here. All temptations do not have to fit one of these strategies. The reminder of the diversity in his attacks should stimulate us to arm adequately for our spiritual warfare.

Jesus' Victory

Left to our own devices, we are no match for Satan, but we are not hopeless. The victory over Satan that Jesus has won is shared with us who put our faith in Him. During His earthly life and ministry, Jesus was never defeated by Satan. Speaking of Jesus as our high priest who sacrificed Himself for our sin, the writer of Hebrews declared,

For we do not have a high priest who is unable to sympathize with our weaknesses, but we have one who has been tempted in every way, just as we are—yet was without sin (Heb. 4:15).

The moral perfection of our Lord encourages us to depend upon Him for victory when we meet the temptations of Satan.

Jesus' authority over demons is an integral part of the Synoptic Gospels.[3] Jesus repeatedly expelled demons that were possessing and ruining individual lives. Demons recognized Jesus and His power over them (Mk. 1:23-27; 3:11-12). The teachers of the law who opposed Him nevertheless admitted His power to cast out demons and decided it was by collusion with the prince of demons that He did so. Jesus countered with this argument:

How can Satan drive out Satan? If a kingdom is divided against itself, that kingdom cannot stand. If a house is divided against itself, that house cannot stand. And if Satan opposes himself and is divided, he cannot stand; his end has come (Mk. 5:23-26).

Jesus was assuring His disciples that Satan's complete defeat was sure but would not occur immediately. One of the most inspiring records of life transformation in the Synoptics is that of the demon-possessed man named Legion who had been uncontrollable, living among the tombs, crying out and cutting himself. Jesus ordered the evil spirit to leave the man, and soon after he was sitting quietly before Jesus, dressed and in his right mind (Mk. 5:1-7; Mt. 8:28-34; Lk. 8:26-37). This evidence of Jesus' mastery of evil spirits is a further comfort to us of Jesus' desire to bless us through His power over evil.

The cross and resurrection of Jesus is also the mark of Jesus' triumph

---

[3]For some reason, John does not mention any of Jesus' miracles of demon expulsion.

over Satan. God used the devil-inspired treachery and betrayal that brought Jesus to crucifixion. The false charges, the hatred, the envy, the demand for bloodshed that Jesus endured were all satanically directed. Wicked men demanded that He be crucified. "But God raised him from the dead, freeing him from the agony of death, because it was impossible for death to keep its hold on him" (Acts 2:24). Satan had done his worst. The innocent Lamb had been slain for sinners, but God's love and power were demonstrated by resurrection, revelation to selected witnesses, ascension, and exaltation to His right hand in glory. This was the purpose of Jesus' coming into the world; as John wrote, "The reason the Son of God appeared was to destroy the devil's work" (1 Jn. 3:8). What blessing is ours as disciples in knowing that we face a defeated enemy. Our Savior has already conquered the devil, and even though we must still meet him on the field of combat, the victorious final outcome is already assured to us. This will ultimately be said of us, "They overcame him by the blood of the Lamb and by the word of their testimony" (Rev. 12:11).

The reign of Christ in heaven now is also grounds for our confidence of victory in Jesus for ourselves. The revelation of Jesus Christ which was given to John on the island of Patmos is full of encouragement for contemporary Christians. Jesus said,

Do not be afraid. I am the First and the Last. I am the Living One; I was dead, and behold I am alive for ever and ever. And I hold the keys of death and Hades (Rev. 1:17-18).

To him who overcomes, I will give the right to sit with me on my throne, just as I overcame and sat down with my Father on his throne (Rev. 3:21).

Even so, the fighting is not over. The angry dragon "was enraged at the woman and went off to make war against the rest of her offspring—those who obey God's commandments and hold to the testimony of Jesus" (Rev. 12:17). The fighting continues, but every true disciple has a right to feel secure about the final outcome while battling for victory in every daily skirmish. Paul stated, "The Lord will rescue me from every evil attack and will bring me safely to his heavenly kingdom" (2 Tim. 4:18).

How We Can Win

We, who have assurance of sharing in the final victory of Christ, still need to learn how to win in spiritual warfare. That is why Paul wrote as he did to the Ephesian Christians and why the exhortation has been preserved for us. We cannot choose whether we shall be in a battle zone, for to be alive in this world makes regular spiritual conflict inevitable. "The day of evil comes" (Eph. 6:13). We do have a choice about how we fight and whether or not we win.

The scriptural answer to the question of how we can win against so formidable a foe as Satan is "put on the full armor of God" (Eph. 6:11, 13). That means put all of your trust in God. Do not rely on yourself. You are no match for the devil. Your strength must come from the Lord. He has "mighty power" (Eph. 6:10). His armor includes everything He provides to enable you to fight victoriously.

The pieces of the actual military armor are not so significant but what they represent is. A belt, a breastplate, sandals, a helmet, a shield, and a sword are mentioned. That was ordinary equipment for a Roman soldier of the first century. Truth, righteousness, the gospel of peace, faith, salvation, and the Word of God are essential equipment for disciples always. All of these are from God. Having them and using them produces triumph. You will still be standing when the fighting is over if you are wearing all of the armor of God.

Prayer is also valuable in the conquest of Satan. Reliance on God will be expressed in prayer. How can the person who seldom or never prays claim to be placing faith in the Lord? Prayer is profitable on all occasions. "All kinds of prayers and requests" (Eph. 6:18) are appropriate. Persistence in prayer is valuable and intercession for all saints is urged.

To these ways Paul discussed, I want to add another factor recommended for successful fighting against the devil. Align yourself with other strong Christians. The devil comes against us with many demons. We would be foolish to try to fight evil alone. God has joined us to a company of sincere saints. We need to strengthen one another, to remain in formation, and to close ranks against our common enemy. Be yoked together with believers.[4] The aid of a mentor, discipler, spiritual director, or prayer support group is advisable.

---

[4]See the reverse admonition in 2 Cor. 6:14.

Our battle strategy should not be only defensive. Sometimes we can boldly attack Satan in his strongholds if we fight in the strength of the Lord. Jesus, in cleansing the temple was hitting the devil in his fortification. He drove out the people who were buying and selling and exchanging money there. "It is written," he said to them, "'My house will be called a house of prayer,' but you are making it a 'den of robbers'" (Mt. 21:13). To pay a personal visit, in the Lord's name, to someone who is peddling pornographic material or operating an illegal business to try to persuade him to desist is taking the offensive against evil. Furthermore, whenever we seek to win a lost sinner to faith in Christ, we are carrying the fight to Satan. Growth to maturity should be marked by increasing courage and skill in assaulting the forces of evil, taking the initiative to overcome Satan.

Our Bodies Are Not Evil

A persistent heresy promulgated through the centuries is that the human body is evil. This false teaching is that all matter is corrupt by nature! Only the spirit is good. Since the body is material, it is thought to be incorrigibly evil. This error is addressed several times in the New Testament.[5]

The main Greek word translated "body" is *soma*. Jesus lived in a real body and spoke of it as a temple (Jn. 2:19-21). He became hungry, thirsty, and tired in His body, but He never sinned. His body was not evil. His body died and it was buried. It was mortal but not evil. Another Greek word which sometimes refers to the body is *sarx*, "flesh." When the Fourth Gospel says "The Word became flesh" (Jn. 1:14), the meaning is that Jesus, who is God, lived in a human body. Jesus warned three disciples who went to sleep on their assigned watch, "The spirit is willing, but the body [*sarx*] is weak" (Mt. 26:41). He did not say it was evil, just weak, prone to drowsiness. This is the way Paul uses *soma* in 1 Cor. 9:27, "I beat my body and make it my slave." He is speaking like an athlete who knows that his body must be rigorously disciplined if he is to be able to compete for the prize. The need of each person to gain control of the body so that it functions properly is no indication that the body is inherently evil.

Jesus taught that the body may be full of darkness or full of light (Mt.

---

[5]See Col. 1:16, 22; Gal. 2:20; 1 Tim. 4:1-5.

6:22-23). Individual responsibility for the body is implied. Likewise, Paul exhorted his readers, "Therefore, do not let sin reign in your mortal body, so that you obey its evil desires" (Rom. 6:12). Instead of turning over parts of the body to be used for wickedness, Christians should offer themselves to God and let Him use their bodies for righteousness.[6] One of the Apostle's major appeals is this:

> Therefore, I urge you, brothers, in view of God's mercy, to offer yourselves [*somata* (bodies)] as living sacrifices, holy and pleasing to God—which is your spiritual worship (Rom. 12:1).

Evil desires are not inherent in the body but are a natural part of the life of sinful persons. Thus, life in our bodies gives Satan an opportunity to tempt us through our eyes, ears, sexual desires, hunger, and other sensual and mental faculties. The spiritual struggle that Paul was writing about between himself and his sinful nature led him to cry out for deliverance—"What a wretched man I am! Who will rescue me from this body of death?" (Rom. 7:24). He saw sin at work in the members of his body. *Sarx* is used in this passage to refer to the sinful nature rather than the physical body. A Christian must always be striving against this fleshly, carnal, or sinful nature.

Our view of our bodies and our sinful natures should never cause us to feel less responsible for our decisions. Paul wrote, "Do not use your freedom to indulge your sinful nature" (Gal. 5:13) and "Live by the Spirit, and you will not gratify the desires of your sinful nature" (Gal. 5:16). He described the conflict that goes on in Christians between the Holy Spirit and the *sarx*, sinful nature. The actions produced by the sinful nature having its way are contrasted with the personality traits or Christlike qualities which the Holy Spirit produces.[7] The purpose of this teaching is to urge believers to continue to yield to the Holy Spirit and live a life consistent with His leadership.

Some of the most positive statements that are found in the New Testament concerning the body (*soma*) are located in Paul's exhortation to the Corinthians to abstain from sexual immorality. He stated, "The body is not meant for sexual immorality, but for the Lord, and the Lord for the body . . . Do you not know that your bodies are members of

---

[6]See Rom. 6:13.
[7]See Gal. 5:19-23.

Christ himself?" (1 Cor. 6:15). The disciple in union with his Lord cannot do anything in his body without involving Christ in his action. Also, Paul reasoned, the body of a Christian is a temple of the Holy Spirit and should be used to honor God.[8] A wider application of this principle seems valid. W. M. Carmichael remarked, "Taking care of health and strength is a religious duty, since failing to take care of our bodies is a sin against God."[9]

Maintaining physical fitness should be seen as an important discipline for every disciple. It is a recognition that through our God-given bodies we are able to respond to Jesus and live as He called us to live. Eating and drinking properly can be a mark of Christian devotion. A sufficient amount of recreation or physical exercise has been shown to be essential to the healthy functioning of the body. Prolonged stress is harmful. Of course, smoking and abuse of drugs are injurious. Although the amount of sleep required by individuals varies, adherence to a systematic sleep schedule is beneficial. Many diseases are related to one's lifestyle, and each of us is responsible for making decisions that are consistent with a Christian lifestyle. Is it not wonderful to think that we honor Christ and glorify the Creator of our bodies by simply doing what is healthiest for ourselves? However, even the attempt to do this involves us in spiritual warfare, since Satan is fighting to weaken and overcome us in every way.

Formation of Christian Character

The formation of Christian character is one of the aims for which every conscientious disciple strives. Spiritual formation and character formation are connected in the Christian life. With the help of the Spirit of God and the instruction of the Scriptures we are endeavoring to build a character that will be a reservoir from which we may draw good ethical decisions. To choose to do right because of fear of the punishment for doing wrong is not the most noble response. When the commandments of the Bible are internalized so that we do right because we are right, good Christian character is manifested. We are all influenced by the approval or disapproval of others; but when we select

---

[8]See the entire passage in 1 Cor. 6:12-20.

[9]John Hendrix and Lloyd Householder, eds., *The Equipping of Disciples* (Nashville: Broadman, 1977), 88. W. M. Carmichael is one of 95 contributors to this volume.

the best course of action regardless of the reaction of people whom we admire or fear, we have demonstrated a higher level of motivation and a more sterling character.

I believe Christian character can be so well-established that a person can do the right thing for the right reason most of the time. He or she is never invincible and would be foolish to suppose so. Nevertheless, a consistent life pattern of wise choices can be constructed as a normal expression of maturing in Christ. Never perfect in this life and never incapable of falling into sin, the individual may still become a good person. Is this not the implication of the compliment paid to Barnabas, for instance, when Luke recorded "He was a good man, full of the Holy Spirit and faith" (Acts 11:24)? To be a good person is to have proved oneself to have good character.

A disciple is assigned to work with God and submit to the Spirit in developing Christian character. Let me suggest five ways to work on this assignment.

1. **Strive to keep a good conscience before God and man**. Paul made it a part of his testimony that he did so (Acts 24:16). The holiness and sincerity that are from God made this possible (2 Cor. 1:12). The Apostle urged Timothy to "fight the good fight, holding on to faith and a good conscience" (1 Tim. 1:18-19).
2. **Allow trouble to be a means of strengthening your character**. Paul was explaining how he could happily endure trouble when he wrote, We also rejoice in our sufferings, because we know that suffering produces perseverance; perseverance, character; and character, hope (Rom. 5:3-4). If we did not ever face adversity, it would be very difficult to build fortitude into our character.
3. **Place a high premium on honesty**. Honesty is absolutely essential to noble character. Think on what is true (Phil. 4:8). "Put off falsehood and speak truthfully" (Eph. 4:25).
4. **Keep your commitments**. As a person of integrity and love for others, do what you promise to do. Pay your debts and show up for your appointments. Be dependable. As the proverb says, "The man of integrity walks securely, but he who takes crooked paths will be found out" (Pr. 10:9).
5. **Choose as close friends those whose character you respect**. We tend to become like those with whom we associate most frequently. The values we select are usually those we see exhibited constantly by

those we admire. Purposeful cooperation with the Lord sustained over the years will build the kind of mature character that a Christian needs to be a fruitful disciple.

Summary

Just as every saved person is a disciple at some level of maturity, so every believer is a soldier of Jesus Christ winning spiritual battles against Satan or losing them. No Christian wins all the battles in this life, but each may learn to fight more victoriously. God has provided everything needed for this warfare. He also has revealed the nature of the spiritual enemy and of his attacks. Jesus has overcome Satan and assured His followers of ultimate triumph. While living in this world, however, we may take steps to develop Christian character as a great asset in spiritual conflict.

Study Questions

1. What is meant by the spiritual nature of our warfare?
2. What are some names and activities attributed to Satan in the Scriptures?
3. Can you distinguish between battle areas and satanic strategies and give some examples of each?
4. Are you able to describe the evidence of Jesus' victory over Satan?
5. Could you aid another Christian in knowing how to win in spiritual warfare?
6. How should we view our bodies in regard to temptations to sin?
7. What is the value of having Christian character and how may we form it in ourselves?

SCRIPTURES FOR MEMORIZATION

I. **Fruitful Discipleship**

  Jn. 15:5; 15:8
  Col. 1:10

II. **Lordship**

  Lk. 9:23; 6:46
  Rom. 14:9

III. **The Example of Jesus**

  Mt. 10:24-25a
  1 Jn. 2:6
  Jn. 13:15

IV. **Godliness as a Goal**

  1 Tim. 4:7-8
  Mt. 6:33
  1 Pet. 1:15-16

V. **True Spirituality**

  Mk. 3:14
  Phil. 3:12-14; 4:13

XI. **Love in the Life**

  Jn. 13:34-35
  1 Jn. 4:7; 3:18

XII. **Servanthood**

  Mk. 10:43-44
  Lk. 17:10
  Col. 3:23-24

VI. **The Heart**

  Mt. 12:34b-35; 22:37-38
  Pr. 4:23

VII. **The Disciplines**

  2 Tim. 2:15
  Phil. 2:12-13
  2 Pet. 3:18

VIII. **Prayer**

  Mt. 7:7-8
  Phil. 4:6
  Lk. 18:1

IX. **Study of Scriptures**

  Ps. 119:11
  2 Tim. 3:16-17
  Jn. 8:31-32

X. **Participation in Church**

  Heb. 10:25
  1 Tim. 3:15
  Acts 2:42

XIII. **Disciplemaking**

  Mt. 28:18-20
  Acts 1:8; 14:21-22

XIV. **Spiritual Warfare**

  Eph. 6:10-11
  2 Tim. 2:3
  Acts 24:16

SELECTED BIBLIOGRAPHY

Adsit, Christopher B. *Personal Disciple-Making*. San Bernardino: Here's Life Publishers, 1988.

Bloesch, Donald G. *The Crisis of Piety*. 2d ed. Colorado Springs: Helmers & Howard, 1988.

Boice, James Montgomery. *Christ's Call to Discipleship*. Chicago: Moody, 1986.

Bonhoeffer, Dietrich. *The Cost of Discipleship*. New York: Macmillan, 1953.

_____. *Life Together*. New York: Harper, 1954.

Bridges, Jerry. *The Practice of Godliness*. Colorado Springs: NavPress, 1983.

Coppedge, Allan. *The Biblical Principles of Discipleship*. Grand Rapids: Asbury Press, 1989.

Cosgrove, Francis M. *Essentials of New Life*. Colorado Springs: NavPress, 1978.

_____. *The Essentials of Discipleship*. Colorado Springs: NavPress, 1982.

Eliot, Elizabeth. *Discipline: The Glad Surrender*. New York: Fleming H. Revell, 1982.

Foster, Richard J. *The Celebration of Discipline*. San Francisco: Harper & Row, 1978.

_____. *The Challenge of The Disciplined Life*. San Francisco: Harper & Row, 1985.

Fromm, Erich. *The Art of Loving*. New York: Harper & Row, 1956.

Griffiths, Michael. *The Example of Jesus*. Downers Grove, IL: InterVarsity, 1985.

Hamblin, Robert L. and William H. Stephens. *The Doctrine of Lordship* Nashville: Convention Press, 1990.

Hendrix, John and Lloyd Householder, eds. *The Equipping of Disciples*. Nashville: Broadman, 1977.

Hodges, Zane. *Absolutely Free*. Dallas: Redencio Viva, 1989.

Holcomb, Daniel. *Costly Commitment*. Nashville: Convention Press, 1978, Revised edition, 1987.

Hull, Bill. *Jesus Christ Disciplemaker*. Colorado Springs: NavPress, 1984.

Kelsey, Morton T. *Caring: How Can We Love One Another?* New York: Paulist, 1981.

Kuhne, Gary W. *The Dynamics of Personal Follow-Up*. Grand Rapids: Zondervan, 1978.

MacArthur, John. *The Gospel According to Jesus*. Grand Rapids: Zondervan, 1988.

MacDonald, Gordon. *Ordering Your Private World*. Nashville: Thomas Nelson, 1984, 1985.

Maston, T. B. *Walk as He Walked*. Nashville: Broadman, 1985.

Merton, Thomas. *Love and Living*. New York: Bantam Book, 1985.

Miles, Delos. *Evangelism and Social Ministry*. Nashville: Broadman, 1988.

Miller, Calvin. *The Table of Inwardness*. Downers Grove, IL: InterVarsity, 1984.

Moore, Waylon B. *New Testament Follow-Up*. Grand Rapids: Eerdmans, 1963.

O'Connor, Elizabeth. *Journey Inward, Journey Outward*. New York: Harper & Row, 1968.

Ortiz, Juan Carlos. *Disciple*. Carol Stream, IL: Creation House, 1975.

Richards, Lawrence O. *A Practical Theology of Spirituality*. Grand Rapids: Zondervan, 1987.

Ryrie, Charles. *So Great Salvation*. Wheaton, IL: Victor, 1989.

Schweizer, Eduard. *Lordship and Discipleship*. London: SCM Press Ltd., 1960.

Stedman, Ray C. *Body Life*. Glendale, CA: Regal Books, G/L Publications, 1972.

Warren, Richard. *12 Dynamic Bible Study Methods*. Wheaton: Victor Books, SP Publications, 1981.

Watson, David. *Called & Committed: World-Changing Discipleship*. Wheaton: Harold Shaw Publishers, 1982.

Webb, Lance. *Disciplines for Life*. Nashville: The Upper Room, 1986.

Whitney, Donald S. *Spiritual Disciplines for the Christian Life*. Colorado Springs: NavPress, 1991.

Wilkins, Michael J. *Following the Master*. Grand Rapids: Zondervan, 1992.

Willard, Dallas. *The Spirit of the Disciplines*. San Francisco: Harper & Row, 1988.